Creativity, Innovation and the Fourth Industrial Revolution

The most important goals for an organization in the Fourth Industrial Revolution will be innovation and enhanced performance. Creativity is a means for promoting these goals – a creative person is a productive person who uses all their resources to attain specific goals. Da Vinci Creativity should be understood as being focused on improving performance both at individual and organizational levels. Traditional organizations can be hierarchical, and thus rigid, at a time when the external environment is undergoing very rapid change. The aim of this book is to present an organizational model that develops leaders who are able to cope with the demands of the Fourth Industrial Revolution.

In light of the increasing levels of innovation being experienced in society around us, *Creativity, Innovation and the Fourth Industrial Revolution: The da Vinci Strategy* offers an organizational theory that can be applied in the Fourth Industrial Revolution. This book will be of interest to researchers, academics, and students in the fields of leadership, strategy, and technology and innovation management.

Jon-Arild Johannessen is a Professor of Leadership at Kristiania University College, Oslo, Norway.

Routledge Focus on Business and Management

The fields of business and management have grown exponentially as areas of research and education. This growth presents challenges for readers trying to keep up with the latest important insights. *Routledge Focus on Business and Management* presents small books on big topics and how they intersect with the world of business research.

Individually, each title in the series provides coverage of a key academic topic, whilst collectively, the series forms a comprehensive collection across the business disciplines.

The Innovative Management Education Ecosystem
Reskilling and Upskilling the Future Workforce
Jordi Diaz, Daphne Halkias and Paul W. Thurman

Management and Labor Conflict
An Introduction to the US and Canadian History
Jason Russell

Creativity, Innovation and the Fourth Industrial Revolution
The da Vinci Strategy
Jon-Arild Johannessen

Performance Measurement in Non-Profit Organizations
The Road to Integrated Reporting
Patrizia Gazzola and Stefano Amelio

Risk Management Maturity
A Multidimensional Model
Sylwia Bąk and Piotr Jedynak

For more information about this series, please visit: www.routledge.com/
Routledge-Focus-on-Business-and-Management/book-series/FBM

Creativity, Innovation and the Fourth Industrial Revolution
The da Vinci Strategy

Jon-Arild Johannessen

NEW YORK AND LONDON

First published 2023
by Routledge
605 Third Avenue, New York, NY 10158

and by Routledge
4 Park Square, Milton Park, Abingdon, Oxon, OX14 4RN

Routledge is an imprint of the Taylor & Francis Group, an informa business

Library of Congress Cataloging-in-Publication Data
Names: Johannessen, Jon-Arild, author.
Title: Creativity, innovation and the fourth industrial revolution : the da Vinci strategy / Jon-Arild Johannessen.
Description: New York, NY : Routledge, 2023. |
Series: Routledge focus on business and management | Includes bibliographical references and index.
Identifiers: LCCN 2022030394 | ISBN 9781032371825 (hardback) | ISBN 9781032371832 (paperback) | ISBN 9781003335726 (ebook)
Subjects: LCSH: Creative ability. | Organizational change. | Technological innovations. | Industry 4.0.
Classification: LCC BF408 .J44 2023 | DDC 153.3/5--dc23/eng/ 20220729
LC record available at https://lccn.loc.gov/2022030394

ISBN: 978-1-032-37182-5 (hbk)
ISBN: 978-1-032-37183-2 (pbk)
ISBN: 978-1-003-33572-6 (ebk)

DOI: 10.4324/9781003335726

Typeset in Times New Roman
by MPS Limited, Dehradun

Contents

Figures

Foreword

We write this book in light of the increasing levels of innovation being experienced in society around us. At the present time, on the threshold of the Fourth Industrial Revolution, many people believe that creativity and innovation will be the most important processes for wealth creation in this new era. The Fourth Industrial Revolution will be characterized by artificial intelligence (AI), intelligent robots, intelligent informats, intelligent algorithms, and the Internet of Things (IoT). This kind of high-technology future will promote cascades of innovations. Many of these innovations will result in socio-economic crises. This is because in many contexts, the new will wipe out the old. As a result, old competences will become surplus to requirements. Meanwhile, it will take time to develop new ones. In the time lag between old competences being rendered superfluous and new competences being developed, many people will experience personal crises. Society will experience institutional challenges and crises of many kinds, both social and economic. In order to shorten this time lag, and the most serious negative consequences of the Fourth Industrial Revolution, there will be a focus on creativity and a demand for ways to promote processes of innovation. This focus on creativity and innovation has been our motivation for writing this book. The method we utilize is known as conceptual generalization (Adriaenssen & Johannessen, 2015). This method requires us to utilize the empirical findings of other researchers but to systematize and structure their findings in order to develop new knowledge in the form of analytical, conceptual, and empirical models, as well as hypotheses and theories that may be useful when put into practice.

1 Da Vinci creativity

Introduction

A leader has an important role in liberating both their co-workers' and their subordinates' creativity (Capra, 2013). In the external environment that employees will encounter, creativity will be an ever more important factor, because of the rate of change and the levels of turbulence and complexity in the knowledge society (Dong et al., 2017).

A leader has a responsibility to facilitate more creative environments in their organization, both because such environments will boost the performance of employees but also because creativity will be taken as a given for mastering the challenges of the knowledge society (Csikszentmihalyi, 2002, 2013).

Creativity cannot be timetabled, but it should be incorporated into the way a leader organizes work in their organization. What we describe here is a strategy whereby a leader can organize and promote creative processes. We have given this strategy a name: da Vinci creativity (Da Vinci, 2005, 2006; Isaacson, 2017). What interests us is how a leader can promote creativity in an organization as a whole (Mauzzy & Harriman, 2003).

If a leader succeeds in developing da Vinci creativity, the organization will experience improved levels of innovation and performance (Galland, 2014). In such a work environment, workers will experience increased levels of engagement and will be motivated to use their powers of creativity and innovation (Capra & Luisi, 2014). Performance will improve, both among individual employees and systemically for the organization. The employees' work environment will be improved and the organization will achieve its goals more easily (Hanson, 2016).

The creativity we are investigating is not artistic in nature. Rather, we are concerned with how a leader can promote creativity in an

DOI: 10.4324/9781003335726-1

organization as a whole. If the leader is successful, creativity will permeate every level of the organization: the individual level; team level; the entire organization internally; and the organization's relationship with the external environment (Heckscher & Adler, 2007).

Da Vinci creativity will permeate everyday activities at individual organizations, promoting ideas generation and making the organization competitive with the flow of information and media entertainment to which the employees are exposed when not at work (Johannessen, 2018). In this context, 'competitive' means competitive in relation to the pressure of information that employees encounter outside the organization. The guiding vision must be that employees view creativity and innovation as interesting and exciting (Johannessen, 2020). The most important goals for an organization in the Fourth Industrial Revolution will be innovation and enhanced performance. Creativity is simply a means for promoting these goals. A creative person is a productive person who uses all their resources to attain specific goals (Csikszentmihalyi, 2013; Johannessen, 2020a). Da Vinci creativity should be understood as being focused on improving performance both at individual and organizational levels (Dong et al., 2017; Johansson, 2004).

There is no 'correct' way to develop da Vinci creativity. However, there are various processes that may be useful, and various techniques that can be applied (Wolfrik Galland, 2014).

This chapter is designed to present a conceptual model for the structure of the remainder of this book. With the help of this model, individual leaders can shape their organizations to make creativity part of everyday life for everyone working at the organization.

The general problem, research questions, and the structure of this book

The general problem we are investigating in this book is: How can we utilize da Vinci's creative thinking to promote innovation in the Fourth Industrial Revolution?

In response to this general problem, we have developed four research questions:

RQ1 How can we utilize da Vinci's strategy to promote innovation in the Fourth Industrial Revolution?

RQ2 How can we utilize da Vinci organizational structures to promote innovation in the Fourth Industrial Revolution?

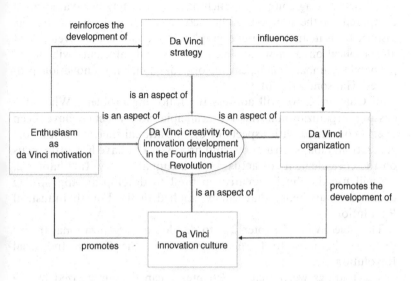

Figure 1.1 Da Vinci creativity for promoting innovation in the Fourth Industrial Revolution.

RQ3 How can we utilize da Vinci's culture of innovation to promote innovation in the Fourth Industrial Revolution?

RQ4 How can we utilize enthusiasm as da Vinci-style motivation to promote innovation in the Fourth Industrial Revolution?

This book is structured according to the model shown in Fig. 1.1.

The structure of this book

In Chapter 2, 'The da Vinci strategy', we will examine the research question: How can we utilize da Vinci's strategy to promote innovation in the Fourth Industrial Revolution?

The organizations that just continue with the old ways of leading and organizing, which led to success in the traditional industrial society, will, in the Fourth Industrial Revolution, find that success will be replaced by failure (Johannessen, 2020a; Morris, 2015). Past history and more recent times are both full of examples of such strategic failures: FASIT, Kodak, and Nokia being just three examples. As a general rule, when the new collides with the old, something innovative will emerge, such as Instagram, the recently established photo-sharing

4 *Da Vinci creativity*

social networking company, which has a completely new value chain compared to the long-established company, Kodak, which has its historic basis in analogue photography. In the future, the development and application of new intelligent robots and informats will, in all probability, impact management, organization, and innovation processes (Hanson, 2016: 6).

In Chapter 2, we will address the following problem. When discussing organizational theory, academia and practice have been overly concerned with aspects of organizational theory, such as organizational maps, structures, and processes but have had little focus on the core elements of actual organizational theory. In Chapter 2, we will use da Vinci's creative method to develop an appropriate organizational theory that can be applied in the Fourth Industrial Revolution.

The objective of Chapter 2 is to develop an organizational theory that can be used to foster innovation in the Fourth Industrial Revolution.

The findings we present in Chapter 2 can be summarized by the following points:

- The traces we leave behind as individuals, organizations, and societies are not so much our knowledge, but the innovations we have created from our knowledge.
- The 'dreamer' is just as important as the 'realist' and the 'critic' in a team, department, or organization.
- The 'dreamer' should have a central place in modern and innovative organizations, equal to that which the CFO and the strategy director have had in traditional industrial organizations.
- In an age characterized by the development and application of artificial intelligence and intelligent robots, as well as by cascades of innovations, bureaucracy and positioning in social hierarchies will hinder value creation.
- As we move into the Fourth Industrial Revolution, there will be a greater need to focus on climate goals, sustainable goals, and the moral/ethical aspects and ecological consequences of the extraction of raw resources, production, distribution, and consumption of products/services.
- The ability to combine knowledge from different domains and fields is at the core of da Vinci organizational structures.
- It is the desire to make a difference that really makes a difference that drives the organizing process in da Vinci organizational structures.

In Chapter 3, 'da Vinci structuring for innovation', we will examine the question: How can we utilize da Vinci organizational structures to promote innovation in the Fourth Industrial Revolution?

The underlying problem to which we will attempt to find a solution is: traditional organizations are too hierarchical, and thus too rigid, at a time when the external environment is undergoing very rapid change. The objective of the chapter is to develop an organizational model that develops leaders who are able to cope with the demands of the Fourth Industrial Revolution.

The findings we present in Chapter 3 can be summarized by the following points:

- Traditional organizations are too hierarchical, and thus too rigid, at a time when the external environment is undergoing very rapid change.
- A breakthrough can be the first step on the road to collapse unless one has clarity of purpose for one's actions.
- Da Vinci leaders inspire others due to their clarity of purpose.
- The objective of da Vinci leadership is to promote what the organization is intended to achieve.
- Having a clear purpose also has a significant advantage, in that one also becomes aware of what one should not spend time and energy on.
- Strategy and technology are necessary pre-conditions for the development of da Vinci organizational structures and da Vinci leaders, but they are not sufficient pre-conditions. On the other hand, clarity of purpose is the crucial sufficient pre-condition.
- Da Vinci organizational structures are not about employing the most intelligent people but are instead about designing a structure that gets as many people as possible to participate in developing the organization's ideas.
- One of the main pillars of the da Vinci organizational structure is making the customers, users and community where the organization is located into the organization's most important and most critical resource.
- Flocking is the most important factor to understand in order to ignite the flame of innovation in an organization.

In Chapter 4, 'da Vinci's culture of innovation', we will examine the following research question: How can we utilize da Vinci's culture of innovation to promote innovation in the Fourth Industrial Revolution?

The underlying problem to which we are attempting to find a solution is: people often oppose change and hinder the development and application of innovations. The objective is to develop frameworks, models, and methods that can promote the development of an innovation culture in organizations as we move into the Fourth Industrial Revolution.

The findings we present in Chapter 4 can be summarized by the following points:

- Organizations are both complex and complicated at the same time.
- Self-organization is based on clear and basic rules.
- An emergent is something qualitatively new, which emerges in social systems, when we move from one level to the next.
- Following a few simple basic rules can lead to complex social behaviour.
- Synchronizing knowledge can result in spontaneous creative processes.

In Chapter 5, 'Enthusiasm as da Vinci-style motivation', we will examine the following research question: How can we utilize 'enthusiasm as da Vinci-style motivation' to promote innovation in the Fourth Industrial Revolution?

The problem to which we are attempting to find a solution is: Traditional motivational psychology is only helpful to a small degree when attempting to understand motivational factors in modern knowledge organizations. The purpose is to design an action plan aimed at developing enthusiasm and motivation in knowledge organizations.

The findings we present in Chapter 5 can be summarized by the following points:

- The success of organizations in the future will to a large degree be determined by their ability to bring creative people on board.
- Employees who feel they are being 'seen and heard' will tend to be more engaged and perform better; consequently, recognition and respect of employees will be important tools in the leader's toolbox.
- Enthusiasm and commitment are crucial factors that positively affect creativity, performance, and the achievement of an organization's purpose.
- The enthusiastic and mindful person is 'present in the moment'. This person is also optimistic and has a positive image of the future.

- 90% of the factors that are crucial to success stem from the attitude one has to challenges and problems.
- Be authentic and say yes to fewer things.
- If you are going to put together a really creative group, then you should search for people who have a basic optimistic attitude, and who think they can solve problems.

This book's ethical values

Every organization functions in accordance with known and unknown principles. Some principles are universally applicable, however. An organization's ethical values constitute one of these basic principles (Morris, 2015). Accordingly, every organization must develop a few clear and simple ethical principles that will determine its governance. These principles must be so simple and so few that everyone in the organization can understand clearly how these principles apply to their everyday work. This is important because such principles should have practical implications for our actions. (Krugman, 2017). For example, an organization could adopt three basic values: respect, responsibility, and dignity (RRD). Everyone in the organization could be presented with an item of jewellery, keyring, or something similar, bearing the letters RRD to symbolize the organization's basic values. Even though respect, responsibility, and dignity are not always easy values to adhere to, the RRD jewellery item or keyring would be easy enough for employees to keep with them at all times.

The employees would thus have tangible and visible reminders of their shared basic values. These reminders would serve as sources of inspiration in the employees' everyday activities. Various levels of feedback could also be provided in relation to these RRD values. Such feedback could relate to the idea of continually experimenting with opportunities to improve adherence to these three values (Perry-Smith & Mannucci, 2017).

The da Vinci creativity is about nurturing unresolved ideas

De Vinci creativity has nothing to do with being smart, intelligent, or capable. A person's creativity can far outstrip their intelligence (Michalko, 2001: 2). Leaders who are working with da Vinci creativity will always keep a particular problem area in focus. They will try to encourage colleagues and employees to put forward as many per-spectives as possible concerning this particular area. Some perspectives will be simple, some conventional, while others may be unique. Our point is that simple solutions can be developed into unique solutions if they are framed in new ways. This is why it is just as important to encourage people to put forward simple suggestions as 'unique' ones. Simple suggestions have the advantage that they are easy to understand.

It is the ways in which these simple suggestions are framed that will determine their utility in practice. A leader's willingness to treat all suggestions with the respect they deserve will send signals back to the suggestion-makers that their contribution is valued. At the individual level, such signals will be inspiring and motivating. Where there is failure to frame a simple idea in such a way that it becomes unique, the failure lies with the leadership team, not with the person who made the suggestion.

It is a simple matter to manage an idea that everyone thinks is a good idea. It is even easier to crush an idea that has not been fully developed. However, it is difficult to develop an unfinished idea, take care of it, give it nourishment, and provide opportunities so it can be developed into a robust idea. It is the latter that da Vinci creativity targets: to nourish the unfinished idea (Nicholl, 2005). There will always be enough people who will take credit for the fully developed idea that everyone thinks is good, even though they may have tried to nip the idea in the bud as it sprouted.

The greatest obstacle to the development of new ideas is our habits, our habitual way of thinking, and our mental models. Deliberately breaking our habits or framing them in a new way will always result in something creative and new. In other words, we need to be constantly on the lookout for alternative ways of tackling problems and challenges, and look for emerging opportunities.

If we are to have the opportunity to promote creativity in an organization, it is a necessary precondition that we have a large variety of ideas. The reason for this is that the organization's environment is always rapidly changing, turbulence is great, and the resulting complexity is also great. When the complexity is great, an organization needs to adapt to the changes that are taking place in the outside world (Stroh, 2015). To accomplish this, a large pool of ideas will be needed, since some of the ideas will never reach fruition. The demand for creativity is directly related to the complexity of the world around us. The greater the complexity of the world around us, the greater will be the need for internal creativity, in order to adapt to the changes that are taking place (White, 2001).

A good rule of thumb regarding creativity and innovation is that if someone says that an idea is unworkable, not valid, not needed, and so on, then it is highly probable that it is precisely this idea that can be developed and turned into a gold mine. In many contexts, being creative means that you have to sail against the wind of current trends. The history of creativity has countless examples of this being true (Michalko, 2001: 4–5).

When an idea is accepted as a good idea, we should be on the lookout for overlooking other ideas, because in such a situation we tend to keep to the accepted idea and ignore many other emerging ideas that could have given better results. In other words, we tend to become transfixed on the one single idea and neglect emerging ideas. In such a situation where a good idea has been chosen, one should make sure to accelerate the idea generation process in order to increase the diversity of possible ideas (Balague & Elmoukliss, 2021). Figuratively, when one door is about to close, you should open other doors and windows to allow enough oxygen into the room. This is in analogy to the selection processes in nature, where variation is a basic principle. The theory of evolution is based on natural selection, and always on the basis of there being a large variety to select from. If the supply is limited, the quality of the results will be reduced. This may also be likened to the creative process. We need to develop 'blind variation' and natural selection to develop creative ideas, says Campbell (1960). Blind variety enables one to create something new and innovative; this can be promoted by analogous thinking and by what De Bono (1995) terms 'parallel thinking'.

In analogy thinking, with regards to organization, one can choose an organizational model from another applicable area, which one believes represents optimal organization. Using analogy, one can select from the chosen area in order to develop an organization model for a business or company. Stafford Beer (1985) adopted this approach when he developed his Viable System Model (VSM); his chosen area was the human brain, which he believed represented an optimal organization of a living system; he then transferred ideas regarding the organization of the human brain, and applied them to a model that can be utilized in the organization of businesses and social systems.

'Parallel thinking' means, as the term suggests, that one places ideas next to each other, without focusing on one particular idea (Bono, 1995: 36). Adversarial stances are not allowed when considering the individual ideas that are presented. The possible consequences of the various ideas are considered, with those ideas metaphorically lying parallel next to each other on the table.

In other words, the so-called adversarial approach of being for and against various ideas has no validity in parallel thinking. Parallel thinking is used today by several prestigious companies around the world; moreover, it is also used by a wide range of educational institutions, spanning from primary to higher education. It is also used in all kinds of businesses, ranging from small local businesses to large global corporations (Bono, 1995).

Some reflections upon da Vinci creativity

Different perspectives provide different solutions. In the same way, different competencies provide different inputs for solving a problem (Balague & Elmoukliss, 2021). When one considers a problem, a challenge, or an opportunity in different ways, this will increase the creative diversity from which one can draw. This is fundamental to all creative thinking, and can be used in various problem areas such as in a strategy process (Capra, 2013).

It is largely our own habits, routines, methods, and mental models that become so fixed that our way of thinking limits our room for action. Our original creativity becomes a stumbling block because we have invested too much psychologically in one or only a few methods. By putting together a team in an organization that has different competencies, problem-solving perspectives, and backgrounds, we can increase our scope of creative thinking and action (Balague & Elmoukliss, 2021).

When our scope of thinking and action increases, we are able to reach a new understanding of how a problem may be solved. This creative approach involves looking at a challenge from several perspectives, framing it in different ways, looking for differences and similarities with similar challenges, bringing out different types of causes, and also focusing on different reasons.

However, we should keep in mind that there is a qualitative difference between cause and reason. There does not have to be a specific cause of a particular event, but there may be many good reasons why it happens anyway. When we distinguish between cause and reason, it is the room for reflection that we have in focus, i.e. how we reflect on how we think (Csikszentmihalyi, 2013). For example, in the 'reflection room', we may use linear thinking. Linear thinking literally moves forward like a line in a sequential order with both a starting and an end point. In other words, linear thinking is so-called cause-and-effect thinking, where we usually ask the question: What is the cause of ---? Circular causality, on the other hand, is non-linear and involves the causal and reciprocal relationships between events and phenomena, and, amongst other things, involves identifying patterns that bind events and phenomena together.

Patterns and da Vinci creativity

The examination of patterns is always interdisciplinary, i.e. the more perspectives from which a phenomenon or problem is examined, the greater will be the probability of gaining insight into the underlying pattern, and thus the possibility of intervening in order to change the pattern (Harman, 2013).

The point of studying patterns in an organizational context is that we live in a social system of which the organization is a part, and we thus contribute to creating the pattern(s) that we will later uncover. It is thus the context of which an organization is a part that provides the premise for how we can act in a situation.

When a problem arises in an organization, such as bullying, the bullying may be said to be a part of a larger social context than the specific organization. How we solve the problem, on the other hand, does not depend on us considering the larger context, because an organization as a system can develop its own identity, values, and norms, even if influenced by the values and norms in the external world of which it is a part. The development of an organization's values and norms is one of the leader's most important tasks. The leader develops these values and norms, even if he/she does not intend to do so; that is, the leader also communicates by not communicating or not acting. It is thus impossible not to communicate in social systems. Different types of values and norms will result in different behaviour within an organization; for example, a certain type of values and norms may result in the emergence of bullying in an organization. If bullying exists in an organization, this will reduce the degree of freedom the organization has to develop employee learning. If we can uncover some pattern connections, then we will also be able to intervene where a problem occurs within a pattern (Klein, 2019).

When you develop a pattern to deal with a problem or a challenge, it will be simpler to avoid habitual logical notions regarding causality, because innovation may more easily be integrated into a pattern that is revealed, than into contexts that remain hidden. Regarding patterns and contexts, one needs to learn how to play around with ideas, without being bound by rules and logical contexts (Krugman, 2017). Ignoring logic can lead to creative solutions that no one saw before. For example, one can choose to view an organization as being completely disconnected from the larger system of which it is part, and then say that the organization needs to solve its problems as if it existed alone on a desert island without contact with the outside world. Everyone knows this is not possible. However, it is often the case that one can find creative solutions by ignoring so-called logic. In other words, by breaking the pattern of which the organization is part, and then defining which norms and values you want to adopt in such a context. By such a manoeuvre, you will be changing the rules of the game in the reality in which you operate, and introduce new rules as if you had full control over all events. This is obviously wrong from every conceivable professional point of view. However, it is not certain that everything that immediately seems wrong will not lead to the desired results. It is also possible that such an approach can affect the larger system of which the organization is part, in the next round (Laszlo, 2008).

Changing patterns and contexts can create new patterns and contexts that have a locomotive effect on the larger system of which the organization is a part. In the game of chess the rules are fixed. You cannot change the rules in chess during the game if you want to maintain a good relationship with your opponent. However, an organization is not governed by fixed rules like those of chess. In an organization, it is first and foremost communication that functions as a social mechanism, initiating change processes (Arnold, 2017). In communication, some rules are fixed, other rules can be changed regularly, while other rules can be changed without any regularity, but changed by decisions that are made (Boulton, et al., 2015).

If you wish to change social processes in an organization, you need to find out which rules can be changed, and what will change when you change these rules. This can be done by the leader of the organization. The leader can decide, within given limits, which behaviour is desired, and which behaviour is not desired (Capra, 2010). By implementing such a decision, right down to the micro level in the organization, the leader can change the norm basis and influence behaviour. The point in this context is that micro-management can have macro consequences (Janis, 1982). By 'macro' we mean in this context that we view the whole organization as a closed system. We are aware of the fact that this is an erroneous representation, and that the organization is obviously not a closed system. However, adopting such a perspective can nevertheless have major positive or negative consequences. In other words, when the leader acts as if the organization is a closed system, different measures will be implemented than if the organization is viewed as being part of a larger whole (Luhman, 1990).

The theoretical basis for this approach is that our perceptions can create real changes, which in turn can influence the development of new perceptions, or, as expressed by Bateson: "We create the world that we perceive". If we express this in a more complex form, we can say that identifying patterns is an attempt to constitute the present moment in time in all its facets.

To understand patterns, one needs to capture social reality through a fundamental playful attitude. If you fail to gain insight into the patterns of which you are part, you will become subject to the rules of a game developed by others. Understood simply, this may be expressed as follows: If you do not design your own plan, you will fall into someone else's plan (Johannessen, 2020).

In the same way that the organization of information can create new information, and new knowledge can illuminate our own lack of knowledge, understanding patterns can create points of intervention for change. An important point about patterns is that if you change one variable in a social context, then the whole pattern will change. However, if one does not have adequate insight into the pattern, un-intended consequences may easily occur as a result when changes are made (O'Reilly & Tushman, 2011).

The technique is to look for variables that belong to the same pattern group because these have relationships to each other and will affect each other if one of the variables changes. The acid test of whether variables are related to each other is whether one variable can be used to explain another variable. However, pay special attention to so-called 'explanatory principles' (Bateson, 1972). According to Bateson in his book, *Steps to an Ecology of Mind,* 'explanatory principles' can facilitate a smooth flow in communication because the communicative partners have a common concept to which they can relate. As illustration, he refers to the word 'instinct', which when used as part of an explanation often does not really explain anything at all (1972: 38).

Against this background, patterns may be viewed as being nothing more than a system of hypotheses. So how do we develop hypotheses? In *Steps to an Ecology of Mind*, Bateson has a dialogue with his daughter where this is expressed clearly:

Daughter: "'Daddy, do you mean that Sir Isaac Newton thought that all hypotheses were just made like stories?'
Father: 'Yes – precisely that.'
Daughter: 'But didn't he discover gravitation? With the apple?'
Father: 'No, dear. He invented it'" (1972: 39).

In some cases, it is possible to develop hypotheses, in other cases, it is not always possible. It is therefore important to distinguish between different groups of ideas.

Even when we work with patterns, it is only an aspect of a phenomenon into which we gain insight. However, it is the relationship between the part and the whole, between emerging concepts and established concepts that creates that which is innovative (Dong et al., 2017). This is what Bateson (1972: 75) means by: "the double habit of mind", and which is the theoretical basis for understanding patterns and contexts. The following quote from Bateson (1972: 89) explains the procedure: "The point is that the first hunch from analogy is wild, and then, then I (... can) begin to work out the analogy". This approach can be used by anyone seeking to develop creativity in an organization.

By utilizing analogies we are able to create something new. An analogy can function as the first triggering step towards creating the whole. This part-whole process is important to understand, in order to create a pattern. In other words, you create patterns, rather than discover them. In the latter case, one would need to have omnipotent knowledge. In the same way that one creates hypotheses, one can also create patterns. By creating patterns one is able to uncover relationships (Johannessen, 2021).

Weick does something of the same with his concepts 'retention, selection, enactment'. To understand these concepts, Weick provides an explanation: "how can I (the actor) know what I think (retention) until I see (selection) what I say (enactment)". Our point here is that one needs to illustrate relationships and patterns in circular models before one can understand what one really means (Capra, 2013). One thus selects something from a specific problem area – consequently, deliberately leaving something else out, and focusing on the parts of what one has selected. Finally, one abstracts some relationships, which one believes to be part of a pattern. Selection, focusing, abstraction is the logical sequence in the development of patterns. One should also be aware of the fact that this process creates breaches in the relationships. In other words, one creates something that one has to relate to at a later point in time.

Starting with a wild analogy, loosely formed terms and concepts, and then bringing the analogy more into focus, shaping the concepts into denser structures and the terms into rigorous analytical tools, can provide an opening for a creative process. This relationship between analogies and developing concepts on the one hand, and the search for rigorous models and unambiguous concepts on the other, involves a relationship between the possible and the certain that we also find in DeBono (1995: 96–130), where, in the creative process, he distinguishes between:

- Opportunity and certainty
- Design versus analysis
- Creating and discovering
- Change versus stability.

It is the scope of opportunity that is made visible on the left side in the above concepts, while what is probable is expressed in the concepts on the right side. The constant interaction between the possible and the probable creates an opening for creativity and pattern understanding.

An approach that Bateson (1972: 85) proposes in order to test the loose thinking that emerged from the analogy is to divide the problem area into a matrix. The horizontal part deals with the main 'logical' parts of the problem area, such as the organization of a business, the business's economic processes, the integration of ethnic minorities, the integration of people with disabilities, and so on. The analytical concepts you have developed are then inserted into the vertical part. You then evaluate each concept in each cell in the matrix in order to examine whether they are valid in relation to the analogy you have developed.

It is the mutual modifications, i.e. opening, closing, opening, closing, that will prevent one from prematurely freezing a concept. This approach is similar to DeBono's concept of lateral thinking or parallel thinking (1995). If we freeze concepts prematurely, then we will tend to develop bipolar characteristics, a type of dualistic opposites. In Western thinking, dualism may be related to dialectics. DeBono (1995) makes a clear distinction between dialectics and parallel thinking, saying that while parallel thinking may trigger creativity, dialectical thinking is important for analysis.

Da Vinci creativity does not require the actors involved in the process to agree on the goals to be achieved. Weick (1979: 91) expresses the following: "All they ask of one another at these initial stages is the contribution of their action". It is the interaction through co-creation that gives the desired results, not agreement on the goals. It is the connection between the possible, the probable, and the practical that creates this interaction, not agreements on goals.

Concluding remarks on da Vinci's creativity

Unexpected relationships can have unintended consequences, because we often have too narrow a perspective on the phenomenon or problem with which we are dealing. We exclude relationships and focus on partial solutions. We do not integrate the aspect of time lag into our thinking, and we do not place sufficient emphasis on threshold values, i.e. that it is precisely 'the last drop that made the glass overflow' or 'the straw that broke the camel's back'. In da Vinci creativity, the basic approach is to focus on points of intervention, i.e. we are primarily interested in how to approach a problem. We can then analyze the basic causes, and discover the underlying patterns. In the everyday life of an organization, it is the points of intervention we should focus on; that is, it is the triggering causes and the associated reasons that can lead the system into the critical situations on which the leader should focus.

References

Arnold, DP. "Introduction to Part I: Early Development and Their continued Repercussions." In *Traditions of Systems Theory*, edited by DP Arnold, 3–10. London: Routledge, 2017.

Adriaenssen, D and J-A Johannessen. "Conceptual Generalization: Methodological Reflections. A Systemic viewpoint." *Kybernetes*, 44, no. 4 (2015): 588–605.

Adriaenssen, J-A and J-A Johannessen. "Prospect Theory as an Explanation for Resistance to Organizational Change: Some Management Implications." *Problems and Perspectives in Management*, 14, no. 2 (2016): 84–92.

Alligood, KT, TD Sauer and JA Yorke. *Chaos: An Introduction to Dynamic Systems*. London: Springer, 1996.

Ashby, R. "Design for a Brain." *Electronic Engineering*, 20 (1948): 379–383.

Ashby, R. *Design for a Brain*. New York: Wiley, 1952.

Balague, C and M Elmoukliss. *From Open to Crowd Innovation*. London: ISTE, 2021.

Beer, S. *Diagnosing the System for Organizing*. London: Wiley, 1985.

Bono, D. *Parallel Thinking*. New York: Penguin Books, 1995.

Boulton, JG, PM Allen, and C Bowman. *Embracing Complexity*. Oxford: Oxford University Press, 2015.

Bunge, M. *Fractals in Science*. London: Springer, 2013.

Campbell, DT. "Blind Variation and Selective Retention in Creative Thought as in Other Thought processes." *Psychological Review*, 67 (1960): 380–400.

Capra, C. *The Hidden Connections*. New York: Flamingo, 2010.

Capra, F. *Learning from Leonardo*. San Francisco: Berret-Koehler, 2013.

Capra, F and PL Luisi. *The Systems View of Life: A Unifying Vision*. Cambridge, UK: Cambridge University Press, 2014.

Carone, TE. *Future Automation: Changes to Lives and to Businesses*. New York: World Scientific, 2019.

Chenowelth, E. *Civil Resistance*. Oxford: OUP, 2020.

Csikszentmihalyi. M. *Flow*. New York: Rider, 2002.

Csikszentmihalyi. M *Creativity, the Psychology of Discovery and Invention.* New York: Harper, 2013.

Da Vinci, L. *Da Vinci Notebook.* London: Profile Books, 2005.

Da Vinci, L. *Leonardo da Vinci: The Complete Works.* London: David & Charles, 2006.

Dong, L, Y Gong, J Zhou, and J-C Huang. "Human Resource Systems, Employee Creativity, and Firm Innovation: The Moderating Role of Firm Ownership." *Academy of Management Review*, 60, no. 3 (2017): 1164–1188.

Ford, M. *The Rise of the Robots: Technology and the Threat of Mass Unemployment.* London: One World, 2016.

Galland, RW. *Leonardo da Vinci: Puzzle Codex.* New York: Carlton Books, 2014.

Hanson, R. *The Age of EM: Work Love and Life, When Robots Rule the World.* Oxford: Oxford University Press, 2016.

Harman, J. *The Shark's Paintbrush: Biomimicry and How Nature Is Inspiring Innovation.* New York: White Cloud Press, 2013.

Heckscher, C and PS Adler. "Introduction." In *The Firm as a Collaborative Community*, edited by C Heckscher & PS Adler, 1–8. Oxford: Oxford University Press, 2007.

Henderson, H. *Edward Lorenz: Climate, Chaos and the New Science.* London: Chelsea House Publishing, 2012.

Isaacson, W. *Leonardo da Vinci.* London: Simon & Schuster, 2017.

Janis, IL. *Group Think.* New York: Houghton Mifflin, 1982.

Johannessen, J-A *The Workplace of the Future: The Fourth Industrial Revolution, the Precariat and the Death of Hierarchies.* London: Routledge, 2018.

Johannessen, J-A. *Building the Innovation Economy.* London: Emerald, 2020.

Johannessen, J-A. *Automation, Innovation and Work: The Singularity Innovation.* London: Routledge, 2020a.

Johannessen, J-A. *Ethics, Innovation, and Artificial Intelligence: Challenges in the Fourth Industrial Revolution.* London: Routledge, 2021.

Johannessen, J-A. and H Sætersdal. *Automation, Innovation and Work.* London: Routledge, 2020.

Johansson, F. *The Medici Effect, Breakthrough Insights at the Intersection of Ideas, Concepts & Cultures.* Boston: Harvard Business School Press, 2004.

Kenis, A and M Lievens. *The Limits of the Green Economy.* London: Routledge, 2015.

Kim, WC and R Mauborgne. *Blue Ocean Strategy, Expanded Edition.* Boston: Harvard Business Review Press, 2015.

Kirzner, S. "The Theory of Entrepreneurship in Economic Growth." I CA Kent, DL Sexton & KH Vesper (Ed.). *Encyclopedia of Entrepreneurship.* Englewood Cliffs. N.J: Prentice Hall, 1982.

Klein, N. *On Fire, the Burning Case for a Green New Deal.* New York: Allen Lane, 2019.

Krugman, P. *Doughnut Economics: Seven Ways to Think Like a 21st-Century Economist*. New York: Random House Business, 2017.

Kurzweil, R. *The Singularity Is Near*. London: Penguin, 2005.

Kurzweil, R. *The Age of Spiritual Machines: When Computers Exceed Human Intelligence*. London: Penguin, 2008.

Laszlo, E. *The Chaos Point*. New York: Piatkus, 2006.

Laszlo, E. *Quantum Shift in the Global Brain*. Rochester, Vermont: Inner Traditions, 2008.

Luhman, N. *Essays on Self-reference*. New York: Colombia University Press, 1990.

Mauzzy, J and R Harriman. *Building an Inventive Organization*. New York: Creativity Inc., 2003.

Michalko, M. *Cracking Creativity: The Secrets of Creative Genius*. Berkeley, Ca: Ten Speed Press, 2001.

Morris, I. *Foragers, Farmers and Fossil Fuels: How Human Values Evolve*. Princeton: Princeton University Press, 2015.

Nicholl, C. *Leonardo da Vinci: Flights of the Mind*. London: Penguin, 2005.

O'Reilly, CA and ML Tushman. "Organizational Ambidexterity in Action: How Managers Explore and Emploit." *California Management Review*, 53, no. 4 (2011): 5–22.

Perry-Smith, JE and PV Mannucci. "From Creativity to Innovation: The Social Network Drivers of the Four Phases of the Idea Journey." *Academy of Management Review*, 42, no. 1 (2017): 53–79.

Pickering, A. *The Cybernetic Brain*. Chicago: The University of Chicago Press, 2010.

Piketty, T. *Capital in the Twenty-First Century*. Boston: The Belknap Press of Harvard University Press, 2014.

Piketty, T. *Chronicles: On Our troubled Times*. London: Viking, 2016.

Raworth, K. *Doughnut Economics, Seven Ways to Think Like a 21st Century Economist*. New York: Random House, 2018.

Schumpeter, J. *History of Economic Analysis*. Oxford: Oxford University Press, 1954.

Schumpeter, J. *Business Cycles*. New York: Porcupine Press, 1989.

Schwab, K. *The Fourth Industrial Revolution*. Geneva: World Economic Forum, 2016.

Senge, P. *The Fifth Discipline*. New York: Doubleday, 1990.

Shipler, D. *The Working poor*. New York: Vintage, 2005.

Standing, G. *The Precariat: The New Dangerous Class*. New York: Bloomsbury Academic, 2014.

Standing, G. *A Precariat Charter*. London: Bloomsbury, 2014a.

Stroh, DP. *Systems Thinking for Social Change*. New York: Chelsea Green Publishing, 2015.

Sunstein, CR. *How Change Happens*. Cambridge, Mass: The MIT Press, 2019.

Tversky, A and D Kahneman. "Judgment Under Uncertainty: Heuristics and Biases." *Science*, 185 (1974):1124–1131.

Tversky, A and D Kahneman. "The Framing of Decisions and the Psychology of Choice." *Science*, 211 (1981): 453–458.

Tversky, A and D Kahneman. "Extensional versus Intuitive Reasoning." *The Conjunction Fallacy in Probability Judgment, Psychological Review*, 90 (1983): 293–315.

White, M. *Leonardo da Vinci: The First Scientist*. London: Abacus, 2001.

Wolfrik Galland, R. *The Leonardo da Vinci puzzle Codex*. London: Carlton Books, 2014.

Zycher, B. *The Green New Deal*. New York: AEI, 2019.

2 The da Vinci strategy for innovation

Key points in this chapter

- The traces we leave behind us as individuals, organizations, and societies are not so much our knowledge, but the innovations we have created from our knowledge.
- The 'dreamer' is just as important as the 'realist' and the 'critic' in a team, department, or organization.
- The 'dreamer' should have a central place in modern and innovative organizations, equal to that which the CFO and the strategy director have had in traditional industrial organizations.
- In an age characterized by the development and application of artificial intelligence and intelligent robots, as well as by cascades of innovations, bureaucracy and positioning in social hierarchies will hinder value creation.
- As we move into the Fourth Industrial Revolution, there will be a greater need to focus on climate goals, sustainable goals, and the moral/ethical aspects and ecological consequences of the extraction of raw resources, production, distribution, and consumption of products/services.
- The ability to combine knowledge from different domains and fields is at the core of da Vinci organizational structures.
- It is the desire to make a difference that really makes a difference that drives the organizing process in da Vinci organizational structures.

Introduction

It is our perceptive and imaginative ability that can stimulate the creation of the new from colliding innovations. Our perceptions stem from processing our observations. However, our perceptions are

DOI: 10.4324/9781003335726-2

intellectualized and theorized, and in a sense detached from practical contexts. By identifying observed patterns and conducting a process of abstraction, we can facilitate theorization. Further, one can think in analogies in order to develop concrete models, usually conceptual analytical models that show the relationships between some key elements. The first three phases of this process: observation, abstraction, and thinking in analogies may be understood as a theoretical exercise. The next step in this process is called transformation, where the theoretical points are transformed into practical relevance. This approach is referred to here as the Leonardo da Vinci method for developing colliding innovations.[1]

Our perception of the world is a creative process where we can create concepts and patterns between concepts at different logical levels. Our imaginative capabilities can also result in the creation of concrete objects, which do not yet exist in the world. Our five senses contribute to our perception of the outer world, that is, our visual (seeing), auditory (hearing), tactile (touch), gustatory (taste), and olfactory (smell) senses. However, our perceptions and ideas are also subjected to an intellectual process, that is, through memory and imagination, for instance, by making associations between various elements. The capacity to imagine is often associated with people with special creative abilities. We might even propose here that our imaginative ideas and perceptions are just as true, or perhaps even more true, than so-called 'reality' and fact-based knowledge, because our imaginative ideas can create a reality which others then investigate in the 'real' world. For instance, Einstein's theories often emerged from his thought experiments, such as his theory of relativity (Frappler, 2015). After his imaginative construction of the theory, physicists then proceeded to verify the theory in the 'real' world, and apply it in more practical contexts (Hawking, 2018).

Our imagination is a powerful instrument for creating that which does not yet exist in the world. We suggest here that leaders should let people daydream – daydreams can be the starting point for what at a later point in time turns out to be practical and useful. It is when people can no longer dream and hope for something better, that we should be afraid. We should encourage people to use their abilities to imagine what is possible, without putting any restrictions on thoughts, feelings, or creative powers. The Fourth Industrial Revolution demands creativity, ideas, dreams, and a free imagination that is not bound by the 'slow fields of history'.

The da Vinci strategy is not locked into fixed structures, hierarchies, or flat structures. The da Vinci strategy takes ideas as a starting point

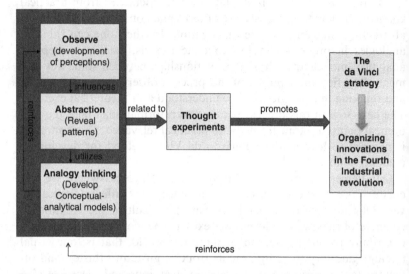

Figure 2.1 Leonardo da Vinci's method for a new innovation strategy in the Fourth Industrial Revolution.

for strategic development and can be developed in any organizational structure. This is where the difference between organizational theory and organizing theory is expressed. Da Vinci strategy is linked to organizing theory, not organizational theory.

In this chapter, we will examine the following question: how can we utilize da Vinci's strategy to promote innovation in the Fourth Industrial Revolution?

Fig. 2.1 provides both a visual representation of the introduction, and of how the rest of this chapter is organized.

The rest of this chapter will provide a description of the elements shown in Fig. 2.1.

Observe

In the observation process, one can attempt to develop an idea by conducting a thought experiment, gaining insight into a phenomenon, acquiring an understanding of how the parts are connected to the whole, and of how the whole affects the individual parts (Capra, 2013). Another way of carrying out the observation process is to examine what one knows about the phenomenon being observed, what one knows that one does not know, what one does not know that one knows, and finally what one does not know that one does not know.

The latter is of course an impossible task, but it is probably precisely here that the creative new can emerge (Capra & Luisi, 2014).

The whole purpose of this observation process is to become one with the phenomenon so that the phenomenon almost becomes a part of oneself. In this context, becoming one with the phenomenon may be related to Csikszentmihalyi's 'creativity and flow' (2002; 2013). The observation process is both an inductive, deductive, and intuitive thought process, where none of these elements take precedence. The observation process becomes creative when our emotions, feelings, and intellectual processes function together as a whole. This is when it is possible to achieve creative results (Csikszentmihalyi, 2013). Creative observations rarely or never emerge from logical-mathematical deductions. They emerge from leaps over logic, from paradoxes, wild associations, and logical flaws (Dong et al., 2017). We are often taught to separate thinking from our feelings and emotions, to be rational and rigorous. In practice, this means that we are taught not to be creative observers who can create something new but instead to carry out logical deductions that an intelligent robot can do a thousand times better than us (Hanson, 2016). We should do what we have the opportunity to master, where we can make a difference, where we do not have to compete with intelligent robots, where we have a burning desire to make a difference that really makes a difference. These are areas where we are in an emotional dialogue with ourselves, when we can feel the hair rising on the back of our necks out of sheer excitement and enthusiasm. Those areas of interest where our feelings and emotions are involved are most likely those areas where we can make a difference, where we can master something, and where we can become good at something. This is where we can stand out from others, and differentiate ourselves from the intelligent robots (Johannessen, 2020, 2020a).

The starting point for creative observation is that all forms of knowledge are interlinked. Prioritizing one form of knowledge over another is the same thing as abandoning knowledge. On the other hand, the creative observation process can start with one form of knowledge, for example a new idea, and then the visualization or model can be developed subsequently. Our initial model or visualization will be incomplete or underdeveloped, and so will virtually always end up being changed or modified. For instance, the *da Vinci Notebooks* are full of different perspectives of the same phenomenon (Da Vinci, 2005, 2006). As a result of such a process, something that is similar, or something that shares some features with what you are observing, can come to be integrated into the new version. What materializes is never a copy, but something that shares some features with the original version. If we observe a starfish, for example, and watch what happens if a starfish loses one of its arms, we will see that both the original starfish and the severed arm can regenerate into complete starfish. If this regenerative principle were applied to organizations, it could be relevant in many different contexts. We could envisage the occurrence of a starfish-like dividing up process where an organization is growing too large to be managed effectively as a single unit. The part that is left behind could regenerate the original functions of the organization. We could also envisage the application of a starfish-like regeneration process where entrepreneurial activities emerge within a long-established organization. As an organizational principle, the starfish principle could replace all the attempted strategies at streamlining in growing organizations, which often just adds more bureaucratic and administrative processes. In such a context, what often happens is that productivity declines, because what the organization has been designed to do gets less attention. The starfish strategy is to develop many small 'tents', so that one can quickly reorganize when the external environment or circumstances require it. At the same time, these small tents have a linked structure, so one can benefit from both the economies of scale and small-scale operations.

In creative observations, concepts are at first undeveloped and ambiguous. It is then important that these concepts are not 'frozen', because this will stop the creative process. There are no monolithic processes in organizations, although they may seem to be so to an untrained eye. For example, leadership is not the same as organizing and vice versa. Of course, there are relationships between leadership and organization, but they are two different phenomena. This is one of the reasons why new leaders often carry out a re-organization, make changes, create new positions, and so on. In this way, the new organization becomes closer to the leader's control zone. Even the language we use about leadership is different from the language we use about organization.

We cannot 'see' or observe concepts. We may have a mental understanding of a concept, but we cannot 'see' them. The point here is that leadership and organization are concepts, and organization should be understood on a different level from the logical rational. If not, the result will be structural incompetence.

In other words, it is not so much logical and rational thinking that fosters innovative processes, but imaginative and creative thinking. The point in this context is that knowing is different from understanding. One may have a great deal of knowledge about the individual parts of a phenomenon, but this does not mean we have a complete understanding of the phenomenon as such. Knowing is different from understanding, just as knowing and understanding are different from creating that which is new and innovative. In the Fourth Industrial Revolution, the emergence of cascades of innovations will be the norm. Therefore, the three domains: knowing, understanding, and creating the new should be integrated, so that part-whole and context-understanding become the norm in competence development. It seems reasonable to assume that contextual understanding will be more important than fact-based knowledge at a time when cascades of innovations are entering the market, and where innovation seems to be the most important competitive parameter, and the most important factor in value creation processes.

The traces we leave behind as individuals, organizations, and societies are not so much our knowledge, but the innovations we have created from our knowledge. The da Vinci strategy takes this statement as a premise and organizes businesses and social systems based on this assumption: What we create is more important than what we know. The point here is that what was once an idea can be evolved into products and services through known and unknown processes. In other words, innovations are materialized from ideas; it is inspiration and ideas that are the starting point for innovative processes. If we take this assumption as our premise, then we need to organize in such a way that we increase opportunities to create the innovative new in organizations. In other words, the 'dreamer' is just as important as the 'realist' and the 'critic' in a team, department, or organization. We need to organize our businesses so that we can relate to the dreamer's ideas, this also concerns the realists and critics. It is not the critics, or analyses of the realists, that create value for a company or organization, but the turning of ideas into invoices. Consequently, modern and innovative businesses should be organized so that the 'dreamer' has a central place, equal to that which the CFO and the strategy director have had in traditional industrial organizations. A 'dream director' may sound too eccentric, but in an organizational context, the importance of having a director of creativity and innovation is something on which most people can agree. Knowledge without ideas is meaningless from a practical perspective. However, ideas without in-depth knowledge can lead to the development of knowledge. It is the combination of knowledge and ideas that is the driving force behind innovation. Ideas, dreams, knowledge, creativity, and innovation will be the drivers of change in the Fourth Industrial Revolution.

Da Vinci organization is the result of ideas and dreams that are realized. However, such a way of organizing can be experienced as pure chaos, because known structures will continuously change. The stable element will be the purpose that the system is designed to accomplish.

The question here is: What is the system designed to do? The system is not designed to establish hierarchies, departments, positions, and layers upon layers of managers and administrators. These are phenomena which we mainly associate with traditional industrial organization, where bureaucracy was appropriate. In an age characterized by the development and application of artificial intelligence and intelligent robots, and with cascades of innovations entering the market, all bureaucracy and positioning in social hierarchies will hinder value creation. A new innovation organization model will emerge, replacing the hierarchical organization. In practice, this will mean that organization will involve a continuous process where dreams, ideas, knowledge, and creativity are all important elements in the development of innovation processes. In order to develop such a new innovation organization, an important premise is that everyone involved adopts common moral and ethical norms, such as showing responsibility, respect, and treating others with dignity. If such moral and ethical norms are adopted by everybody in the organization, then employees will be better equipped to tackle major changes and the fact that the stability of the known structures no longer exists.

We have summarized creative observations in Fig. 2.2.

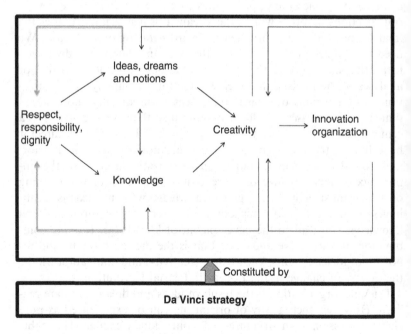

Figure 2.2 Creative observations: An analytical model.

Abstraction

Abstraction is concerned with filtering out, and discarding the elements that we do not need, in order to concentrate on those that we do need. It is this selection process that creates the abstraction. The process of abstraction should attempt to identify a pattern in that which is being observed, which may be related to data, information, assumptions, or the empirical results of others. If one uses one's own empirical results, this is termed empirical generalization. When one uses the empirical results or the assumptions of others in the abstraction process, this is termed conceptual generalization (Adriaenssen & Johannessen, 2015).

The process of abstraction is crucial in order to stimulate innovation processes and create the new. In businesses, this should be organized so that the abstraction process, that is, revealing patterns, becomes as natural as creating a good working environment. A strategy for an abstraction process can be adopted by introducing a few simple investigative steps, by examining where:

1 The relative quality is falling.
2 The relative income is falling.
3 The relative costs are increasing.
4 The relative productivity is falling.
5 The diffusion of innovation is the greatest.
6 New knowledge has the potential to be transformed into new technology.
7 The relative competence is increasing the most.

Based on such investigations, it will be possible to determine where innovations will most probably emerge (Johannessen, 2019, 2019a). This organization of abstraction processes thus has a clear practical utility, because organizations will be able to prepare for emerging innovations, either by being at the forefront of the development themselves or by adapting to what will emerge in the near future (Johannessen, 2020, 2020a). For example, most businesses compete in the market on the basis of low costs and customer satisfaction. Da Vinci organizing of a business, on the other hand, focuses on those areas where few or none are competing, not unlike the so-called 'blue ocean strategy' (Kim & Mauborgne, 2015). However, the difference between a da Vinci organization of a business and a blue ocean organization is that da Vinci organization focuses on the entire creative process from observation, abstraction, analogy-thinking to practical utility, something the blue ocean strategy does not.

The Fourth Industrial Revolution will be characterized by demanding customers that will be in constant motion (Perry-Smith & Mannucci, 2017); that is, customer loyalty is a concept which we associate with the industrial society. In the knowledge society, which is another term for the Fourth Industrial Revolution, customers will be continuously attracted to innovative products and services (Csikszentmihalyi, 2013). Moreover, a growing customer group will also relate innovative products and services to the ethical, ecological, and climate impact aspects of production and sales (Johannessen, 2021). Therefore, it is not low cost alone that will determine the attractiveness of a product or service, but what the low cost entails, or how the low cost has been achieved (Krugman, 2017). For instance, is the low cost achieved by using child labour, employing extremely low-cost labour, or by using production processes that are harmful to the environment? In other words, a company's 'ethical' reputation will have direct consequences for the possible success of a company, more so than today, because, amongst other things, the negative consequences of the climate crisis and environmental pollution created by the industrial society are negatively impacting people's lives today. Consequently, the abstraction processes above involving the seven investigative steps should also include an additional eighth step, that is, an examination of the moral/ethical, climatic, and ecological consequences of extraction, production, distribution, and consumption of the product/service.

In addition to the 7+1 investigative steps mentioned above, the process of creative abstraction can be expanded through the following point. Allow yourself to be inspired, in other words, allow yourself to be overwhelmed by what you observe. This point relates to the idea of our inner child, who sees what is new in everything, including things we have seen before. Allowing yourself to be inspired will manifest itself in enthusiasm. An enthusiastic person will find it easy to lead and inspire others.

The progress of mankind is often viewed as a journey from *mythos* and irrationality towards *logos* and rationality. However, in the journey towards rationality we perhaps lost a lot along the way. Among other things, we lost the ability to imagine how we can create our own reality (Da Vinci, 2006). Today, people with this ability are often dismissed as idealists and dreamers, as though this ability is something negative (Frappler, 2015). Perhaps we have to return to *mythos* in order to re-acquire these lost abilities. Abilities that we used to create the future

we wanted (Isaacson, 2017). In the age of *mythos,* we had constant reminders of what might lie in our pasts and what could follow us into our
futures. However, today, such thinking is often associated with mental
instability. *Logos* has taken control of all our capabilities and made
mythos into something that is only suitable for children, such as the
telling of myths, legends, and tales. This dominance of *logos* and rationality is creating major obstacles to our thinking at a time when
complexity, robotization, globalization, and extreme inequality are
emerging worldwide (Johansson, 2004). Obviously, the Oracle of Delphi
was not logical or rational, but our point is that the Oracle's prophecies
were often realized precisely because people believed in them. The same
is true in the case of an inspired and enthusiastic individual; some people
believe in them and this belief causes things to happen in reality (Morris,
2015). An artistic project can be defined as allowing oneself to be inspired by something or someone: a dream; a distant thought; a butterfly;
a word that might materialize, and so on. *Mythos* can be understood as
part of an artistic process, the act of creating something that doesn't yet
exist in the world. Our point is that the creation of such things is not the
sole province of artists, but of all of us. We create new things by imagining that they are possible, and then having faith in these possibilities.
And then through this inspiration, we can engage others in our project.
To do so, however, we must liberate ourselves from the logical and
rational. We should be able to imagine what would happen if a river
flowed through the air, or if one could remove the difference in water
pressure between the seabed and the sea's surface, or the difference in air
pressure between sea level and the upper atmosphere. Could this lead to
the development of a future source of energy? These are the kinds of
flights of fancy that can lift us out of the straitjacket of rationality and
into a world of the imagination. A world where we can observe things
that don't yet exist, but that may be realized in the future.

We can find inspiration and enthusiasm in many places. One example would be in a 'designed mentor', i.e., a mentor that we create for
ourselves, a helper or 'muse' that inspires us to be creative and innovative. In Greek and Roman mythology, the nine Muses inspired
artistic and creative endeavours. In these Muses, we find inspiration,
longing, hope, and creative energy (Nicholl, 2005). Abstraction, on the
other hand, breaks down this energy but at the same time gives it
direction so that it is channelled into more fixed structures. In a way, it
is like first playing with vague thoughts and ideas, and then through a
process of abstraction freezing them into clearly defined structures
(Bateson, 1972). A visitation from a source of energy beyond the realm
of rationality and logic can provide inspiration for creative innovation.

Such a visitation might come in a dream, in a letter from a stranger, when watching a leaf fall from a tree, when hearing the sound of a wolf howling in the distance, when seeing a flock of birds in the sky above, and so on (Amabile, 1983). The important thing is to seize the moment, that is, the moment when 'the visitor knocks on the door'. Otherwise, the visitor will vanish forever and never return, or at least the message they were bearing on that particular occasion. The moment one takes the message from the visitor is the moment when inspiration strikes, when enthusiasm is triggered, and when one allows oneself to be carried away (Capra, 2013).

The process of abstraction is characterized by a spirited curiosity, bordering on the compulsive, and by inspiration and enthusiasm that can result in the bringing of the new into the world. In addition, the ability to engage in lateral thinking also characterizes the process of abstraction (Galland, 2014: 2). It is not only discovering patterns that is the purpose of the abstraction processes but also discovering the patterns that show the underlying structures in the observations that have been made (Isaacson, 2017: 1). This can be expressed as the pattern that connects patterns. To bring this about requires a continuous interaction between the parts and the whole (Isaacson, 2017: 2). The central element in the abstraction process, as in all da Vinci organizing, is driven by connecting knowledge and insights across knowledge boundaries. It is the ability to combine knowledge from different domains and fields that is at the core of da Vinci organizational structures. Moreover, it is the burning desire to make a difference that really makes a difference that drives processes in da Vinci organization. This is Leonardo's approach, which also applies to da Vinci organization: curiosity and intense observation (Isaacson, 2017: 3), and ideas that border on pure imagination. We can all develop these three abilities: curiosity, intense observation, and imagination – they are not reserved for the skilled, nor are they innate, but instead can be learned.

It is the underlying curiosity of what can be improved that drives da Vinci organization. The abstraction process can be based on many different techniques. One can, for example, try to visualize different perspectives of a problem or challenge. The visualization may then provide inspiration for the abstraction process.

Thinking in analogies

Analogies are used to make comparisons and show relationships, often to explain an abstract concept in terms of something that is concrete and easier to understand.

For example, a beehive may be used to explain the abstract concept of business organization; an anthill may be used to explain the division of labour in human society, and so on. Beer used the analogy of a human brain to explain the organizational structure of social systems (1985). Inspiration for an analogy may come from unexpected sources; for instance, the sudden vision of a flock of birds in flight may provide inspiration for an analogy to explain teamwork or collaboration. However, well thought out analogies are usually the result of a long period of hard work focused on a particular phenomenon or problem.

The basic thinking behind using analogies is to imagine the phenomenon 'as if they were' (Root-Bernstein & Root-Bernstein, 1999: 137). If one takes as a starting point organizations, then one may imagine how they could be organized 'as if they were': brains, hearts, bodies, beehives, a flock of birds, a shoal of fish, and so on. Analogy concerns 'a functional resemblance between things that are otherwise unlike' (Root-Bernstein & Root-Bernstein, 1999: 137). Of course, organizations are not literally 'brains', but one can organize them as if they were. In this way, as mentioned, Beer created his 'Viable System Model' (VSM), a model for organizing organizations as living systems, by using the human brain as an analogy (Beer, 1995). However, by comparing the human brain to an organization one of the questions that arises is: is the human brain organized according to some hierarchical principle, or does the human brain just consist of different functions with different tasks? In other words, does one part of the human brain 'lead' the other parts, or is the organization done according to other structuring mechanisms?

An analogy is not intended to show that two phenomena can be directly and truthfully compared. Of course, as mentioned above, an organization is not organized in exactly the same way as the human brain. The point of analogies is not to find 'truthful' comparisons, but to unleash creativity, so as to improve our understanding of a phenomenon or problem, or to create a new and innovative understanding. In other words, analogies help us to create insight into areas where our knowledge has clear shortcomings or needs improvement. For example, we can never 'see' an entire organization and everything that goes on there with the naked eye. Analogies therefore help us to see connections, understand social mechanisms, gain insight into processes, and so on. Analogies also help us to use knowledge developed in one context in another context; for example, knowledge gained from brain research that can be transferred to the field of organizational theory, in order to illuminate various relationships and processes. So how can we transfer this knowledge between different contexts? The answer seems to lie in the point that the ideas that knowledge consists of, and is built around, can be related to a new context and so fertilize the new context with ideas that did not exist before.

The point is that the analogy can act as an instrument for transferring an idea from one context through transformation processes to a new context. The transformation process takes place through the ideas taking different leaps, often through completely random jumps. Specifically, this is done by consciously changing perspective, taking the new perspective as given, and then after a while changing yet again to another new perspective. This conscious shift in perspective results in the original idea being transformed into a usable idea in the new context. In other words, one takes the original idea, dividing it into its smallest meaningful units, and then putting these parts together into a new idea in the new context.

Using an analogy is like entering into a 'foreign country', a country where one doesn't know the language, or what to look for, and one is left to use the analogy in order to find one's way. This may be compared to using a map and compass to navigate unfamiliar terrain. However, the map is imperfect. Accordingly, the map only indicates a few places that can probably be trusted, and it must be amended and made into a better map according to one's acquired experiences. In other words, one is completely handicapped but believes one has an assistive aid with this imperfect map. Metaphorically, the map functions as an analogy. It gives energy to creativity and gradually changes as one's own sureness and knowledge grow.

What we can understand directly in this 'foreign country' is so incomplete that we must study the shadows in order to imagine who or what is casting them. In the thought experiment above, this imperfect map helps us to associate and draw familiar lines into unknown terrain. In this way, a river on the map may correspond with a river in the unknown terrain. After a while, we will be able to fill in the old map with a new point of reference, and slowly but surely create fragments of the new landscape. Through the use of analogies, we see the emergence of some principles of correspondence. This was done by, among others, Stafford Beer, when he used the brain as an analogy for an optimal model for an organization's structure. Thereafter he arrived at some simple and easily understood relational rules, which he used to develop his Viable System Model (VSM).

The analogical process involves observation, conjecture, reflection, and associative thinking. This process allows ideas to develop freely. One looks at similarities and dissimilarities, for example between a brain and how an organization can be structured. One could also use a leaf as the basis for an associative process: how the small veins subdivide towards the outer edges of the leaf, how the process of photosynthesis within the leaf resembles the processing of information within an organization. One can think about the structure of a leaf and the structure of an organization and reflect on the extent to which the branching of a leaf's main vein is organized hierarchically or functionally. The former interpretation argues in favour of a hierarchical organizational structure, while the latter argues in favour of a function-based non-hierarchical structure. One can also think of the structure of a leaf as a system of relationships and then attempt to transfer this interpretation to organizational structures. This approach of using associations is about finding relationships that can be transferred from the original subject of the associative thinking to the target. As mentioned, the structure of a leaf may be likened to that of an organization. The relationships that one transfers can be referred to as relationship 1-n. For example, one could take relationship 1 (e.g. the main vein in the leaf) and attempt to find areas of application within the organization. This could easily result in the assumption that all decisions should follow one general pathway leading from top management down to the organization's operational level. On the other hand, relationship 1 could also mean that all decisions in an organization should be linked to a channel of communication that is so broad and open that all feedback is heard and responses are provided to the feedback from the people working to implement the decisions. As one will understand, this associative process does not provide any set answers as to how one should apply the various relationships. The point is not to provide set answers, but to reflect on similarities and differences in order to reveal a pattern that can be applied when structuring an organization, for example.

When you have little direct knowledge of an area or problem, analogous thinking can lead to creative and innovative answers to questions you are working on. It is thus not our observations that limit us but our ability to see and to use analogies to solve a problem. The analogy we utilize does not necessarily have to be directly related to the problem we are working on, on the contrary. On the other hand, when we have first decided to use a specific analogy, we will of course attempt to relate the characteristics of the analogy we have chosen, and the problem or phenomenon we are trying to say something about, for example, organizing organizations at a time where intelligent robots are taking over more and more tasks and functions from the people in organizations.

Analogy thinking concerns taking an existing phenomenon and applying it in a totally different context. By comparing two phenomena or two objects, or systems of objects, one can highlight functions and elements in which they are thought to have correspondences. Based on the second phenomenon, that is, the phenomenon one is investigating, one attempts to find two or more functions, processes, and so on, that correspond to the analogous phenomenon. One is not attempting to find similarities in the sense of a metaphor, where there is a resemblance of two different things based on a single or a few common characteristics. Metaphors and analogies differ from each other. Analogies can be used to explain various relationships and associations. Metaphors, on the other hand, suggest an image that is meant to show one or more similarities, such as organizations as prisons. One may start with a metaphor in analogy thinking, but one should not stop there, because this does not constitute thorough analogy thinking. For instance, when discussing viable organizations, Stafford Beer takes as his starting point a metaphor comparing an organization to the human brain. However, he moves on from there to show that an organization can not only be likened to a human brain but that the comparison can be used as an explanation for showing how an organization can function like a human brain. In this case, the question in analogy thinking is: how can the functions of the human brain be transferred to the management of an organization? When we compare a human brain to the management of an organization, we are able to uncover functions and processes in the human brain that we can transfer to the organization of social systems and organizations. These processes and functions can be completely new and innovative in the field of organizational theory, such as the five systems in Beer's Viable System Model (VSM). These comparisons are not based on exact numbers or values but emerge through creative processes.

Analogy thinking is widely used in the world of science. Newton used it in his discovery of the law of gravity (Newton's apple analogy). Darwin used analogy thinking to develop the Theory of Evolution (Darwin's analogy of breeding and nature). Other scientists also used analogies extensively when developing their theories, such as Einstein (Theory of Relativity), and Benjamin Franklin's Theory of Electricity.

The point here is that analogy thinking is just as prevalent in science as it is in the world of art. One tries to find connections between the known and the unknown through analogy thinking. It is the thousand associations one can draw from good analogies that give strength to the creative process.

The difference between an analogy and a metaphor can be shown in the following:

- Analogy: Leadership and myths
- Metaphor: Leadership as a dwarf, leadership as a princess, leadership as a troll, leadership as the unearthly, etc. To construct a metaphor from an analogy, you can go into the analogy and draw out something special on which you then focus.

The most effective analogies are those that have passed through one's own senses as a result of one's own experiences, as we have seen in the cases of Darwin, Newton, and Einstein. To arrive at such analogies, thought experiments are crucial.

Thought experiments

Thought experiments have a very high degree of abstraction; however, it is seldom that empirical studies support thought experiments. Thought experiments are largely modelled on perception, analogous thinking, and figurative language.

In Greek philosophy, the thought experiment (*deiknymi*) was used to highlight conceptual correlations. In the history of philosophy, Plato's Cave Allegory is perhaps the most well-known thought experiment. In the history of science, the oldest thought experiment is perhaps Galileo's observations concerning the velocity of falling objects in a vacuum. On the basis of this thought experiment, Galileo rejected Aristotle's law of gravity. Whether or not Galileo transformed his thought experiment into a practical experiment in the Leaning Tower of Pisa is still a topic for discussion among historians of science. In our context, thought experiments are of great interest because they may have major implications for both theory and practice.

In the scientific field, thought experiments have been used by Einstein, Podolsky, and Rosen, among others. In what is referred to as the EPR paradox, the three scientists attempted to show that Heisenberg's uncertainty principle did not provide an adequate explanation in quantum physics. Another well-known thought experiment is Schrødinger's cat.

The importance of the thought experiment for scientific methodology was particularly emphasized by the philosopher and science theorist Paul Feyerabend, and also by the philosopher and science theorist Mario Bunge (1999, 2000, 2001). An important purpose of thought experiments is to apply them as hypothetical scenarios in order to highlight a few key points and to examine the possible consequences of a research question.

A thought experiment may be defined as an experiment in which controlled mental actions are performed by a person in relation to a phenomenon or problem area with the purpose of solving a theoretical or practical problem (Bunge, 1997: 126). However, a thought experiment is not considered to be a genuine scientific experiment as such, but consists of imagining what may happen if certain facts were to occur or if they had occurred (Bunge, 1997: 126). Bunge says of thought experiments (German: *Gedankeneexperimente*) that they, "have no validating force, but they may spark off interesting hypotheses" (Ibid).

A thought experiment may be understood on the basis of the three cognitive processes: *Attribution, association,* and *generalization* (Bunge, 1983: 174).

Attribution is when we attribute a property or a relationship to an object, phenomenon, or problem. For instance, we may see an apple fall from a tree and attribute this to the property of the force of gravity (Newton's thought experiment). Thus, in the process of attribution we see or perceive something, and then conjecture an attributing property; thus we move from sensory perception to the development of concepts through a generalization process. In other words, we move from the empirical level (sensory perception) to a level of abstraction (the concepts) which is not directly linked to the empirical level. This occurs by making conjectures regarding possible relations until at some point we are satisfied, without being certain, that our assumptions are correct. In other words, we shape conceptual relations, and on the basis of this attribution process we develop a thought experiment. In the example mentioned above of the falling apple, Newton is believed to have 'discovered' the law of gravity. Thought experiments are often tested out empirically to substantiate the accuracy of the presumed relations; thus, one of the results of a thought experiment might be a testable hypothesis.

In *association,* different domains are related to each other in order to create something new. For instance, Stafford Beer's Viable System Model (VSM) draws similarities between management and organization and the structure and function of the human brain (Beer, 1995). Association can be carried out in different ways. Associations may be made to natural phenomena; a beehive has a very special form of organization, and a few 'simple rules' that ensure high productivity in the collection of nectar, often called 'the dance of the bees' (Facklam & Johnson, 1992). It is not difficult to imagine how this natural phenomenon may be associated with ideas concerning the design and operation of an effective public or private organization. Associations may take place at various levels and between different types of objects and social systems. However, it is always the phenomenon or the problem area that is the starting point of an association. If, for example, we are interested in how cooperation functions in organizations we may make an association to cooperation in the natural world, such as how bird flocks, schools of fish, swarms of bees, colonies of ants, and so on, work together in order to survive. On the basis of such an association, it would be possible to develop the concept of 'flocking' which could then be applied to the design of conceptual models where 'flocking' was the phenomenon under investigation (for instance, in human organizations). Another example could concern an examination of Schumpeter's concept of creative destruction. In this context, it may be of interest to examine what happens in the years after a forest fire. In this example, destruction is a prerequisite for the growth of new trees (the 'creative new' in Schumpeter's concept). Associations need not be 'true'. The point is that they initiate ideas that can be used in a thought experiment.

There are two types of *generalization*. The first type is based on similar cases which are compared over time and where we attempt to find a pattern, often referred to as a type of inductive generalization. Pavlov's classic conditioning experiment with dogs provides such an example. Dogs were exposed to the sound of a tone shortly before feeding, and after a period of time they would salivate in response to the tone before receiving food.

The second type is based on individual cases, where we look for a transfer of learning or experience; for instance, how a specific organization was able to develop an innovative information and learning system that resulted in an increase in both innovation and productivity. A process of generalization would involve a transfer of experience to other organizations, i.e. they would adopt the same system used in the specific case.

An important purpose of generalization is that we condense information so that we can, for example, quickly infer an effective response from a signal. Generalization helps us to economize our resources; however, it may also lead to inaccuracy.

A conceptual model of the above-mentioned processes in a thought experiment is illustrated in Fig. 2.3.

While experiments might be said to be more important than observations (Bunge, 2014: 121), we can also say that thought experiments are a necessary precondition for real-world experiments.

When developing a thought experiment, we seek to build a bridge between that which is observable and that which is not. While a carpenter measures a length of wood using his/her ruler, a researcher measures by means of indicators, symptoms (e.g. the temperature of a patient), and markers (that which is observable). However, it is that which is not observable that we are really interested in, such as the disease behind a high fever or the tacit knowledge that is possessed by an expert but not

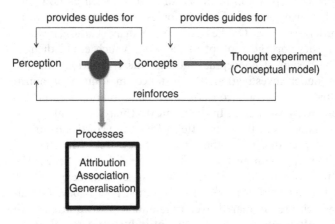

Figure 2.3 A thought experiment as a process model.

by a novice. This understanding concerning indicators is important because in many cases we cannot come directly to grips with a phenomenon or problem. You often have to begin with indicators and key features of the components in a conceptual model (for instance, in a thought experiment).

Conclusion

In this chapter, we have examined the following research question: how can we utilize da Vinci's strategy to promote innovation in the Fourth Industrial Revolution?

The simple answer is that we need to learn to develop conceptual models because these can show us some social mechanisms that affect social processes. By getting to grips with organization processes through the use of conceptual models, we will be able to illustrate relationships of which we previously were not aware.

The relationships between social mechanisms and social processes at the macro and micro levels are shown in Fig. 2.4.

The more comprehensive answer to the research question can be described in terms of how we design conceptual models.

The purpose of conceptual models is to model a problem or phenomenon such that its generic properties are isolated. Further, the purpose is to understand or explain the nature of the phenomenon/problem. Conceptual models can be designed at different levels of abstraction, and relate to the few or many empirical studies that the conceptual model is based on.

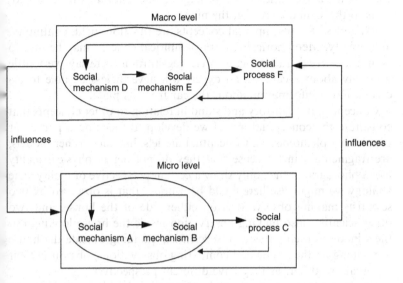

Figure 2.4 Social mechanisms and social processes.

A conceptual model can be applied in order to generate innovative ideas, which may have theoretical and/or practical relevance. This type of model consists – as the term suggests – of concepts. These concepts are made up of components. In the same way that indicators should be developed when measuring the results from practical experiments, we need components and their essential properties in order to say something about the concept inherent to a conceptual model.

Conceptual models are always related to a problem or a phenomenon; without this relation, they would cease to have meaning or purpose. However, it should be noted that concepts and models only capture aspects of reality in relation to the phenomenon or problem we are attempting to represent.

Concepts, however, bear no resemblance to what they represent; they are constructed abstractions, not physical representations. Figuratively, one can say that there is no similarity between a fish and the word 'fish'. There are two types of concepts:

1   Those which **originate** from a process of perception, and
2   Those which **do not originate** from a process of perception.

We may call them empirical and transempirical,[2] respectively. An empirical concept may be understood as being analogous to a map, whereas a transempirical concept may be understood as being analogous to the symbols used on the map.

Examples of transempirical concepts are function, field, continuity, and infinity. Metaphorically, a transempirical concept may be said to be like a car registration plate. A car registration plate says very little generally about a car, but an expert will nevertheless be able to ascertain much information about the car from its plate.

Concepts have a history and stand in relation to other concepts that constitute the conceptual model we develop to focus on a particular problem or phenomenon. Conceptual models, like most other models, are fragmentary in the sense that they do not depict physical reality like a photograph; they only show a certain perspective of reality. The analogy we might use here could be a house that is observed by two scientists making observations on either side of the house, and two other scientists also making observation inside the house looking out the windows on either side. The scientists standing outside the house are talking on the phone and comparing observations; obviously their observations differ, as they have different perspectives.

Similarly, the scientists inside the house looking out into the outside world also report differing views of what they observe. The differing views may not be relative, but they are all real and objective; however, they only reveal aspects of 'reality', from the point of view (perspective) of the individual researcher. This analogy attempts to show that when a researcher observes a problem/phenomenon in the social world, then he/she does this on the basis of three main processes:

1   We select something from a phenomenon or problem area; we also choose to discard much of what is contained in the field of the phenomenon/problem area.
2   What we select is generalized through abstraction processes.
3   In these abstraction processes, that which we have selected is altered and distorted in relation to its origin. This is no more complex than the fact that data differs from information, which again differs from knowledge.

A conceptual model based on this understanding is thus a figurative representation of various relations. The concepts are designed so that they denote a system of components that constitute central key features of the concept. The components have such relationships with each other and give meaning to the concept precisely because of their key features and their relationships.

What has been examined thus far may be summarized in the following points for the development of a strategy for designing conceptual models:

1 Clarify the problem/phenomenon.
2 Develop a precise research question.
3 Define the generic properties of the social universe that is being studied, and determine this in terms of various concepts, such as concepts A, B, and C.
4 Determine the relations between the concepts, by using words such as 'influence', 'reinforce', etc.
5 Decide which components should be included in the concept.
6 Determine the key features of the components.
7 Develop indicators for the key features.
8 Determine the relationships between the components of the various concepts.

The eight points listed above represent the first steps when developing conceptual models. Once this has been done, various strategies may be followed. Points 9–13 provide examples of how to proceed further:

9 Construct an analytical framework (or thought experiment).
10 Develop an analytical model based on the analytical framework.
11 Use the analytical model to examine an empirical context.
12 Develop empirical causal models on the basis of the analysis from point 11 and examine quantitatively an empirical context.
13 Develop and visualize the quantitative relationships emerging from the analysis in point 12.

Notes

1 This approach is taken from the following sources: Capra, 2013; Capra & Luisi, 2014; Nicholl, 2005; White, 2001; Right, 2017; Wolfrik Galland, 2014; Da Vinci, 2006, 2005; Isaacson, 2017; Nathan & Zollner, 2015. For pedagogical reasons, we will not further refer to these sources in the following text.
2 From an epistemological standpoint, there are differing views here. Idealists deny the existence of empirical concepts or say they are dependent on trans-empirical concepts, whereas empiricists deny the existence of trans-empirical concepts. From a 'realism' or systemic perspective, some concepts may be said to have their origins in 'percepts', while others do not.

In the following, due to space limitation and pedagogical considerations, we will not consider the various discussions in the philosophy of science concerning these points. We would, though, like to bring to the reader's attention the important role the philosophy of science and scientific theory play in the formulation of different perspectives, including the development of concepts, conceptual models, and conceptual generalizations.

References

Adriaenssen, D and J-A Johannessen. "Conceptual Generalization: Methodological reflections. A Systemic Viewpoint." *Kybernetes*, 44, no. 4 (2015): 588–605.

Amabile, TM. "The Social Psychology of Creativity: A Componential Conceptualization." *Journal of Personality and Social Psychology*, 45, no. 2 (1983): 357–376.

Bateson, G. *Steps to an Ecology of Mind*. London: Ballantine Books, 1972.

Beer, S. *Diagnosing the System for Organizations*. New York: Wiley, 1995.

Bunge, M. *Exploring the World: Epistemology & Methodology I*. Dordrecht: Reidel, 1983.

Bunge, M. *Foundations of Bio-Philosophy*. Berlin: Springer Verlag, 1997.

Bunge, M. *The Sociology-Philosophy Connection*. New Brunswick, NJ: Transaction, 1999.

Bunge, M. "Ten Modes of Individualism—None of Which Works—and Their Alternatives." *Philosophy of the Social Sciences*, 30, no. 3 (2000): 384–406.

Bunge, M. *Philosophy in Crisis: The Need for Reconstruction*. Amherst, NY: Prometheus Books, 2001.

Bunge, M. *Evaluating Philosophies*. Berlin: Springer, 2014.

Capra, F. *Learning from Leonardo*. San Francisco: Berret-Koehler, 2013.

Capra, F and PL Luisi. *The Systems View of Life: A Unifying Vision*. Cambridge, UK: Cambridge University Press, 2014.

Csikszentmihalyi. M. *Flow*. New York: Rider, 2002.

Csikszentmihalyi. M. *Creativity, the Psychology of Discovery and Invention*. New York: Harper, 2013.

Da Vinci, L. *Da Vinci Notebook*. London; Profile Books, 2005.

Da Vinci, L. *Leonardo da Vinci: The Complete Works*. London: David & Charles, 2006.

Dong, L, Y Gong, J Zhou, and J-C Huang. "Human Resource Systems, Employee Creativity, and Firm Innovation: The Moderating Role of Firm Ownership." *Academy of Management Review*, 60, no. 3 (2017): 1164–1188.

Facklam, M and P Johnson. *Bees Dance and Whales Sing: The Mysteries of Animal Communication*. New York: Sierra Club, 1992.

Feyerabend, PK. *Against Methods*. London: Verso, 2010.

Frappler, M. *Thought Experiments in Philosophy, Science and Arts*. London: Routledge, 2015.

Galland, RW. *Leonardo da Vinci: Puzzle Codex*. New York: Carlton Books, 2014.

Hanson, R. *The Age of EM: Work Love and Life, When Robots Rule the World*. Oxford: Oxford University Press, 2016.

Hawking, S. *Brief Answers to the Big Questions*. London: John Murray, 2018.

Isaacson, W. *Leonardo da Vinci*. London: Simon & Schuster, 2017.

Johannessen, J-A. *Automation, Capitalism and the End of the Middle Class*. London: Routledge, 2019.

Johannessen, J-A. *Historical Introduction to Knowledge Management and the Innovation Economy*. London: Emerald, 2019a.

Johannessen, J-A. *Building the Innovation Economy*. London: Emerald, 2020.

Johannessen, J-A. *Automation, Innovation and Work: The Singularity Innovation*. London: Routledge, 2020a.

Johansson, F. *The Medici Effect, Breakthrough Insights at the Intersection of Ideas, Concepts & Cultures*. Boston: Harvard Business School Press, 2004.

Kim, WC and R Mauborgne. *Blue Ocean Strategy, Expanded Edition*. Boston: Harvard Business Review Press, 2015.

Krugman, P. *Doughnut Economics: Seven Ways to Think Like a 21st-Century Economist*. , New York: Random House Business, 2017.

Morris, I. *Foragers, Farmers and Fossil Fuels: How Human Values Evolve*. Princeton: Princeton University Press, 2015.

Nathan, JN and Zollner, F. *Leonardo da Vinci: Complete Paintings and Drawings*. London: Taschen, 2015.

Nicholl, C. *Leonardo da Vinci: The Fights of the Mind*. London: Penguin, 2005.

Perry-Smith, JE and PV Mannucci. "From Creativity to Innovation: The Social Network Drivers of the Four Phases of the Idea Journey." *Academy of Management Review*, 42, no. 1 (2017): 53–79.

Right, D. *Leonardo da Vinci Biography Bio Book*. London: Independently published, 2017.

Root-Bernstein, R and M Root-Bernstein. *Sparks of Genius*. New York: Houghton Mifflin, 1999.

White, M. *Leonardo da Vinci: The First Scientist*. London: Abacus, 2001.

Wolfrik Galland, R. *The Leonardo da Vinci Puzzle Codex*. London: Carlton Books, 2014.

3 Da Vinci structuring for innovation

Key points in this chapter

- Traditional organizations are too hierarchical, and thus too rigid, at a time when the external environment is undergoing very rapid change.
- A breakthrough can be the first step on the road to collapse unless one has clarity of purpose for one's actions.
- Da Vinci leaders inspire others due to their clarity of purpose.
- The objective of da Vinci leadership is to promote what the organization is intended to achieve.
- Having a clear purpose also has a significant advantage in that one also becomes aware of what one should not spend time and energy on.
- Strategy and technology are necessary pre-conditions for the development of da Vinci organizational structures and da Vinci leaders, but they are not sufficient pre-conditions. On the other hand, clarity of purpose is the crucial sufficient pre-condition.
- Da Vinci organizational structures are not about employing the most intelligent people but are about designing a structure that gets as many people as possible to participate in developing the organization's ideas.
- One of the main pillars of the da Vinci organizational structure is making the customers, users, and community where the organization is located into the organization's most important and most critical resource.
- Flocking is the most important factor to understand in order to ignite the flame of innovation in an organization.

DOI: 10.4324/9781003335726-3

Introduction

A leader's task in developing a da Vinci organizational structure is to make their objectives clear and visible (Collins & Porras, 1994). This will be a necessary, although not sufficient, pre-condition for developing da Vinci leaders in organizations. The motivators are linked to allowing people in the organization, wherever they may be in the organizational hierarchy, to act on instinct and a basic need to want to innovate in the interests of the organization (Dong et al., 2017).

However, this presupposes that the so-called 'rule-breakers' are given the opportunity to operate in the organization (Malhotra, 2020). This may cause tensions within the organization, because the rule-breakers will be a source of 'irritation', and it may also be felt by many that the actions of the rule breakers are creating turmoil. Moreover, the rule-breakers may also come into conflict with the so-called contrapreneurs in the organization, that is, those people who resist change, and who strive to maintain the status quo in order to maintain their position and power within the organization.

Consequently, when irritation and chaotic conditions occur, it is essential that the leadership treat the rule-breakers with the necessary respect and dignity so that their unfinished and unborn ideas are not nipped in the bud (Earls, 2007). Rule-breakers often collaborate in horizontal networks that are not structured hierarchically, which can stimulate the creation of new ideas across established structures (Hansen, 1999). If the leadership can facilitate a positive working environment for the rule-breakers, i.e., those who the contrapreneurs perceive as being 'troublemakers' and 'disruptors', this may trigger positive behavioural changes throughout the organization, resulting in a 'bandwagon' effect. Consequently, this may also stimulate positive developments in the da Vinci organizational structures at various points throughout the organization, as well as in the network between the da Vinci structures in the organization and its surroundings, such as customers, suppliers, competitors, and the authorities.

In this chapter, we will examine the following question: How can we utilize da Vinci organizational structures to promote innovation in the Fourth Industrial Revolution?

We have illustrated the above description in Fig. 3.1, which also shows how we have organized this chapter.

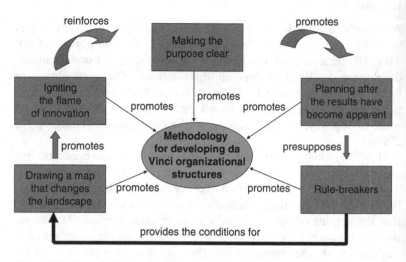

Figure 3.1 A methodology for developing da Vinci organizational structures.

Making the purpose clear

A breakthrough may be the first step on the road to collapse if an organization does not have a clarity of purpose for its actions. Collins and Porras (1994) have shown that having a clear purpose is an important characteristic when distinguishing successful organizations from the rest. As early as 1985, Stafford Beer (1985) developed his model for viable systems, in which he emphasized the importance of purpose, which he termed System 1. Rosabeth M. Kanter (2006) points to 'the communities of purpose', which she views as being crucial for creating a common direction in any social system, and an important criterion for success.

The purpose that drives individuals and organizations to create that which is unique, i.e. 'the difference that really makes a difference' is twofold: Firstly, the organization should have a clear purpose concerning what it is supposed to do, which prevents it from losing its sense of direction. Secondly, part of the purpose is concerned with reaching out beyond the everyday business of an organization, which provides energy and drive to create the extraordinary.

Beer's purpose, and Kanter's 'communities of purpose' (2006), concerns the inner cultural ties that make da Vinci organizational structures pulsate with energy. Purpose is located above the goal, or goals, and is more tangible than the 'vision'.

In the field of research, curiosity often provides strong motivation, but it is not necessarily related to purpose or goal. The purpose of research is often to find answers to appropriate questions. The visions of research can vary, for example, aimed at solving the problem of poverty, the climate crisis, or finding cures for diseases, and so on. Having a clear purpose also has a significant advantage in that one becomes aware of what one should not spend time and energy on. With regard to delivering products to customers, this is termed 'non-value added' activity by Liker (2004), amongst others, and is an important factor in manufacturing that companies such as Toyota pay special attention to. In other words, a non-value added activity is an activity that does not increase value for customers.

Strategy and technology are necessary pre-conditions for the development of da Vinci organizational structures and da Vinci leaders, but they are not sufficient pre-conditions. On the other hand, clarity of purpose is the crucial sufficient pre-condition. Collins (2001: 10–11; 65–90) has shown that although some companies had adequate technology and a clear strategy, they were nevertheless not transformed into successful companies because they did not have a clear purpose.

Purpose drives one's conscious choices. You choose something, and thus also discard something else. Creating da Vinci organizational structures and developing da Vinci leaders requires a clear purpose, because you deliberately discard something that does not create value for customers, or you do not focus on those factors that contrapreneurs feel they need to emphasize in order to maintain their position and power within the organization.

Da Vinci leaders inspire others due to their clarity of purpose. However, as Collins (2001: 13) shows in his research, and which can be transferred to da Vinci organizational structures, the first thing that should be done is to:

1 Get the right people on the bus.
2 Make sure there is no one on the bus who should not be there, i.e., the contrapreneurs.
3 Get the right people in the right seats.
4 Find out in which direction you want to drive the bus (when the first three conditions have been met).

Point 4 is the strategy. The strategy is thus developed after the right people are on the bus, which may be somewhat contrary to more conventional strategic thinking.

An important purpose for da Vinci leaders is to simplify, that is, to make what is perceived as chaotic and highly complex seem simpler. Da Vinci leaders identify the underlying pattern, so others can see what needs to be done. Da Vinci leaders focus on what is important, and choose to ignore things that are less important; one can say that 'first things first' is an appropriate motto for a da Vinci leader.

The people who use da Vinci organizational structures have a clear and unambiguous purpose and direction based on their unique competence and insight into what drives them forward, as well as an understanding of what their fundamental interests are (Dong et al., 2017).

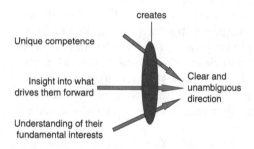

Figure 3.2 The characteristics of people using da Vinci organizational structures.

Referring again to Jim Collins' (2001) bus analogy, the people participating in a da Vinci organizational team or unit should be able to answer the following three questions if they want to get on the bus:

1   What expertise do you have that is unique – regardless of what expertise this is?
2   What really drives you in what you do – whatever this may be?
3   What are your fundamental interests, which causes you to do that little extra that makes others look at you as if you're special, and which enables you to perform at your best?

Those people who want to get on the bus, and take part in da Vinci organizational teams or units, should be able to answer the three questions, because they provide a clear and unambiguous direction for da Vinci organizational structures. However, this does not mean that you know exactly what will emerge from da Vinci organizational structuring. On the contrary, it just means that the right people will get on the bus.

Those people who got on the bus can now be considered to be 'wild cats'. They will seldom or never be ruled through a hierarchy, by a bureaucracy, or by traditional control mechanisms. However, they will let themselves be led towards a specific goal; just as real wild cats can be led by the nose to where you want them to go by laying out a smelly, old fish in their path. In other words, the people in a da Vinci organizational team or unit can be led by using the answers to questions two and three above. We can also say that the analogy with 'wild cats' is also appropriate regarding managing creative knowledge workers – they cannot be controlled but they can be led.

Da Vinci organizational teams and units in the Fourth Industrial Revolution will mainly employ creative knowledge workers. Therefore, it is also crucial to know what drives them and what their fundamental interests are (Johannessen, 2020).

Creative knowledge workers in da Vinci organizational structures are motivated by their fundamental interests, which drive them towards a goal or goals. The goals are related to their unique competence. As mentioned above, this is one of the basic insights of Jim Collins (2001): First, you get the right people on the bus, then you place them in the right seats, then you drive the bus in the right direction. In order to drive fast enough, but not so fast that you cannot navigate the sharp bends in the road, creativity should be maintained, while keeping a clear direction. In other words, it is the balance between creativity and a clear direction that creates da Vinci structures in organizations, provided that the right people are on the bus, and that they are sitting in the right seats.

However, if creativity is given free reign, while direction is unclear, then chaos and conflict may quickly occur, because the 'wild cats' will be chasing different 'fish'. If there is little creativity and the direction unclear, then the organization can go over the cliff with a full portfolio, as was the case with the Swedish office machine company FASIT, Kodak, and many others – these are the dying organizations. If there is little creativity, while direction is clear, one can easily end up where many entrepreneurial organizations throughout history have ended – tangled up in bureaucratic, hierarchical structures, where 'red tape' suffocates the organization. We have illustrated the above description in Fig. 3.3.

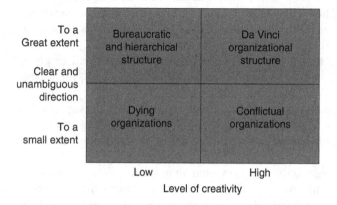

Figure 3.3 Da Vinci organizational structuring.

Planning after the results have become apparent

A significant aspect of da Vinci organizational structures is that adjustments and trimming of the organization are only done after the da Vinci organizational structures have become apparent. This is a point made by Dong et al.: The results drive the process, not the other way around (2017), which turns much of the traditional thinking on its head regarding how to staff and run an organization. In da Vinci organizational structures, one does not plan for results, but one plans the processes once the results have become apparent. Specifically, da Vinci leaders look around the organization and evaluate the various results. People are then organized into various da Vinci teams. Of course, you cannot run the whole organization along these lines, so you start with one part of the organization, and then you slowly but surely follow the same procedure regarding the other parts.

Acting on a gut feeling, and the desire to create something, as well as believing that it is possible, and then acting as if the desire has been fulfilled, is the secret to developing da Vinci organizational structures. Responding to a gut feeling may be related to the idea expressed in Taylor and Labarre's book, *Mavericks at Work,* when they write about the desire to create value for customers (2007: 34), which we can term here, 'the First Law of Mavericks'.

The second law of Mavericks may be expressed as follows: "If you're going to start a company, you better have an idea so radical that most people think it's crazy" (op. cit.).

However, it is important to remember that many ideas that are perceived as being 'crazy' are in fact 'crazy', and will never succeed: a rough estimate is that only one of a thousand ideas will have the potential to succeed (Hamel, 2000; 2007). Therefore, it is also important to relate the two laws to each other: an extreme customer focus and 'crazy' ideas. An extreme customer focus implies interaction skills with customers. 'Crazy' ideas imply contextual competence, i.e., understanding and insight into the part and whole.

'Crazy' ideas are created on an intuitive level rather than by rational analysis. An extreme customer focus, i.e. wanting to create value for customers, is based on existing and potential needs, desires, interests, and preferences of customers. In this context market knowledge and analysis is important. The vibrant life in da Vinci organizational teams and units thus rests on two pillars:

1 'Crazy' ideas
2 An extreme customer-focus

The purpose that connects these two pillars together is a burning desire 'to make a difference that really makes a difference'.

To succeed, these elements are only necessary conditions. The sufficient condition, which i.a. Kim and Mauborgne (2005) have expressed, and which we concretize here in the concept Viking strategy is:

1 You have to go where there is no competition. There is no sense in competing with 'Goliath', as this does not normally lead to success (although it did in the Biblical story).
2 One seeks to solve problems, meet needs and desires that have not yet manifested themselves in the form of demands. This is also reflected in the statement: "We have no interest in competing with anyone" (Taylor & LaBarre, 2007: 38).

We have illustrated the pulse and direction in da Vinci organization structures in Fig. 3.4.

In other words, it is not sharp elbows in the market that is needed to develop da Vinci organizational structures, but rather an eagle eye on customers, away from the established areas of competition, coupled with a burning desire to create value for the customers.

How do we find the right people to be part of a da Vinci team or unit? The following 'cues' say something about these people (Johannessen, 2022), they:

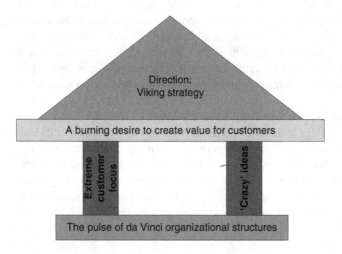

Figure 3.4 The pulse and direction of da Vinci organizational structures.

1   Have a clear purpose of what they want to do.
2   Are constantly seeking to be unique.
3   Are constantly focused on what they are doing at any one time.
4   Are humble and willing to learn from others.

In conclusion, the following question can be asked: What would the organization lose if these people suddenly left?

It is important to remember that when developing da Vinci organizational structures not everyone needs to be an employee; the employees participating in da Vinci teams and units will also have relationships and networks outside the organization. Allowing these networks to actively participate in the development of da Vinci organizational structures will contribute new ideas to the organization. Surowiecki (2005) has shown that if you put together a team of experts, and another team consisting of experts and non-experts, then it is the latter team that will, in most cases, be able to solve problems more effectively.

An open innovation model has been proven to work better than a closed one, because an organization does not necessarily have access to the most skilled people within its pool of employees. However, under the right conditions the best people available can be associated to the organization if they are given access to information and rewarded for results.

Titles, options, salaries, and education are not prerequisites when developing good, 'crazy', or smart ideas. When the market, technology, culture, and social conditions are changing rapidly, other models for the development of innovation are needed. The open innovation model and the 'crowd model' are such models, which have been shown to work effectively in practice (Balague & Elmoukhliss, 2021).[1] The organizational design of a da Vinci team should therefore benefit from this relatively new insight, where one unleashes the creativity of 'the crowd' to develop collaborative innovative solutions to deal with a problem or challenge (Malthotra, 2020).

In today's global competition, innovation models that are 'top-down' managed have little chance of survival, because the dynamics and complexity in social systems are now qualitatively different from the time when such models worked quite well. The idea behind open innovation models and 'crowd' models is to let 'the thousand flowers bloom', as long as they 'sprout in our garden' (Taylor & Labarre, 2007: 75). The main reason for preferring open innovation and 'crowd' models can be expressed by the following statement: "Companies cannot ignore the collective intelligence of the network – the fact that one million people will always be smarter than twenty people" (Taylor & Labarre, 2007: 75).

Da Vinci organizational structures are not about employing the most intelligent people but are about designing a structure that gets as many people as possible to participate in developing the organization's ideas. The pertinent question to ask is: Who has an interest in developing the organization along these lines? The answer is quite simple: Those who daily use and depend on the organization's products and services.

One of the main pillars of the da Vinci organizational structure is making the customers, users, and community where the organization is located into the organization's most important and most critical resource. This also corresponds with open innovation and 'crowd' models. However, this presupposes that the organization makes critical information available to customers. This may at first sight seem intimidating and counterproductive because competitors can then more easily access the information and utilize it. However, in the global knowledge economy, the rate of growth of new innovations will be very high, so only those who have direct access to the 'thousand flowers' will be able to nourish and harvest them in their own garden (that is, keep pace with innovation development). Those who do not encourage this type of development will soon be left with an 'artificial potted plant', figuratively speaking. The metaphor we can use for this participatory structure is the web/internet, which simultaneously fosters decentralized, interconnected, collaborative, and distributed processes. In these processes, knowledge emerges and reinforces innovative processes. Taylor and Labarre (2007: 77) express this in the following way: "For the first time in human history, mass cooperation across time and space, is finally economical". Da Vinci organizational structures aim to utilize this opportunity for the benefit of organizations. What will happen if every company and business takes advantage of this opportunity? Then new knowledge will emerge when different domains of knowledge collide with each other, and what for some was what 'they did not even know they did not know', will become 'something they know they do not know'. From this point, creative knowledge processes can start. The more different kinds of knowledge that are integrated, the greater will be the likelihood of increased creativity and innovation, or in the words of Taylor & Labarre (2007: 95): "—innovations are all about networks.— It is about making connections, combining things, moving things from one domain to another".

We have illustrated da Vinci organizational structure in relation to four main types of innovation models in Fig. 3.5.

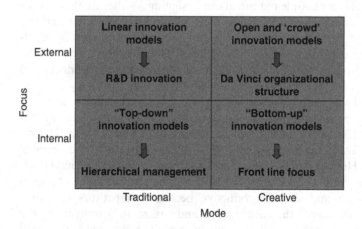

Figure 3.5 Da Vinci organizational structure in relation to four innovation models.

The necessary conditions for developing da Vinci organizational structures

Consumers are continually being given more and more choices, and prices are increasingly being reduced due to global competition and new technology. However, this is not necessarily resulting in increased customer satisfaction. We may term this the 'paradox of increased choices'. One would imagine that greater choice and lower prices would lead to increased customer satisfaction. If it is not especially choice and price that are the determining factors regarding customer satisfaction what is it then? This maybe something as simple as framing regular products and services in the market in a new way. In this context, Starbucks (coffee) and Potbelly Sandwich Shop (sandwiches) provide two good examples. What do such companies have in common that frame regular products and services in a new way?

1 The most important factor is the uniqueness and presentation of the product or service.
2 The customer experience of the product or service that is delivered is the core activity of the organization.
3 The actual product or service comes as a cherry on top of the cake for the customer who experiences something unique.

When a cup of coffee is no longer just a cup of coffee, and a sandwich is no longer just a sandwich, then you have framed the coffee and the sandwich in a new way, which increases customer satisfaction, even if the basic product is more or less the same.

In areas such as telecommunications, education, computers, shopping, and so on, how can one frame products and services in such a way that a product or service is experienced as being something special and unique? The answer is to put the main focus on the actual customer experience and customer relationship, and the secondary focus on the actual product or service.

One of the answers is to frame regular and basic products and services in an innovative way, so that customers can personally relate to what is being offered, so they feel they are part of the development of the product or service. This is where da Vinci organizational structures can connect to the customers by actively engaging them in various creative ways, so that they get a real experience of being involved in developing whatever the company is delivering in the market.

Customers have the feeling of being part of something creative, when products and services are presented as unique, special, and experience-oriented, even if this just concerns basic products and services, such as teaching in schools, public transport, coffee bars, or products in hardware stores, and so on (Syed, 2019). This can easily be achieved if one allows da Vinci organizational structures to develop freely. For instance, what is it that customers want when purchasing a product or service? They want businesses to be accessible and responsive to their wishes (Malhotra, 2020). If this is correct, then businesses should organize their activities around this simple wish. If there are other wishes the customers have, then the businesses should organize their activities around these wishes too.

Customer experience in any business can be summarized with the words, 'easier, simpler, and fun'. In other words, we should:

- Make it easier for the customer.
- Make it simpler for the customer.
- Make the customer experience fun.

The customer experience is a whole that cannot be analyzed by breaking it down into single factors and then summing these up. Neither can a customer experience be transferred to others as information. The customer experience can contribute to identity – the difference that really makes a difference, and can separate one business from another. The challenge when creating an experience for customers does not necessarily involve the presentation and delivery of a product or service but involves relating to the customer in the way that he/she finds most suitable. The customer experience may be about small details that can really make a difference, which are so distinct, that although small, lead to great consequences. It concerns standing out as special at a time when the choices available to customers are very many.

If one were to take supply and demand as a starting point, it would often be quite risky to enter the market at a time when supply is plentiful and customers' choices are almost endless. An important point regarding da Vinci organizational structures is not to take the visible demand as a starting point, but rather the needs, wishes, interests, and preferences of potential customers.

In many businesses, there is an increasing supply, a relatively stable demand, and a very high level of competition. In such a situation, da Vinci organizational structures should connect with the 'smart' customers, and develop products and services together with the customers. Continuing with a 'business as usual' mentality and a strategy that involves 'more of the same' in such a situation will put businesses at risk. The following characteristics can be a starting point for creating that little extra in da Vinci organizational structures:

1 Do what others don't do.
2 Stand out by being different in an area that means a lot to customers.
3 Focus on genuine customer experiences.
4 Allow customers to develop products and services.
5 Having an extreme focus on adapting to the customer.
6 Conceptually tear down the whole organization, and then re-build, while looking for a positive 'spin off' in the process.
7 Post your ideas online and let others contribute creative input.
8 Ensure that what you deliver is also what you stand for in terms of values.
9 Put together a team that is a mix of experts and lay people, where decisions are decentralized and emerge as a compromise.
10 Use the creativity of 'grass roots' movements.
11 Give away knowledge when someone requires it, because you will always get more back in return.
12 Develop products and services that are extreme in a particular field in order to set the scene.
13 Learn from the best in the industry, while also learning from those who really shine in other lines of business.
14 Attend to the needs, desires, interests, preferences, and values of customers.
15 Design lifestyle products.

We have conceptualized the above points in Fig. 3.6.[2]

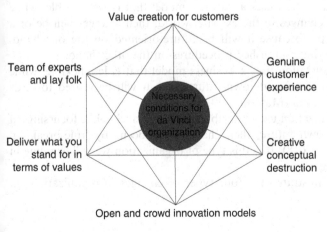

Figure 3.6 Necessary conditions for da Vinci organization.

'Crazy' ideas and an extreme customer focus presuppose that an organization is willing to break established rules and norms. In the next section, we will take a look at these rule-breakers.

Rule-breakers

Change in organizations may be understood in many ways – here we will consider change along two axes. The first axis concerns how an organization adapts to changes in the external world, and an organization's initiative in creating its own future. The second axis may be understood in relation to the extent which an organization operates using a flexible business model (Dong et al., 2017).

The simultaneous existence of a highly flexible business model and a focus on creating an organization's future is often perceived as hazardous by many leaders, because it increases risks and creates a high degree of uncertainty regarding rules and procedures in organizations. Yet, there is much to suggest that it is precisely those organizations that can manage to live with risk and uncertainty that are able to create 'hits' and capture markets, says Farrell (1998).

What we term here 'rule-breaking organizations' are those organizations that use a more flexible business model and focus on creating their own future. It is these organizations that have the prerequisites to develop da Vinci organizational structures (Johannessen, 2021).

When an organization uses a flexible business model, while adapting to changes in the external world, then it will be able to continuously make improvements, because of its focus on cost and quality (Syed, 2019).

If an organization uses a business model that is less flexible, while adapting to changes in the external world, then changes will be of a proactive type, because it will be future-oriented on the one hand, while conserving established procedures on the other hand.

If an organization uses a business model that is less flexible, while focussing on creating its own future, then it will be geared towards structural renewal (Malhotra, 2020).

If an organization uses a flexible business model, while focussing on creating its own future, then changes will occur by 'rule-breaking' (Johannessen, 2018). It is this type of organization we will examine in the following.

We have illustrated the four types of changes in organizations in Fig. 3.7.

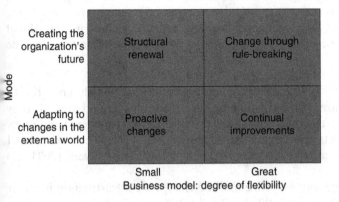

Figure 3.7 Types of changes in organizations.

Rule-breaking organizations have a 'paranoid trait' in the sense that they are continuously alert to others that are trying to push them out of the market. But, this 'paranoid trait' is positive in its consequences, because it means the organization is constantly searching for new and better ways to tackle challenges and problems. The rule-breakers on the level of the individual are coordinated by being synchronized in the sense that they have an extreme customer focus, which integrates all activities and communications in the organization (Balague & Elmoukhliss, 2021).

A rule-breaking organization is not an open system that adapts like a chameleon to its environment. On the contrary, it is open and closed at the same time. It is normatively closed in the sense that it only focuses on creating its own 'world', rather than adapting to changes in the external world. It is cognitively open in the sense that it uses a highly flexible business model (Luhmann, 1995).

While a rule-breaking organization is open and closed at the same time, it becomes integrated as a kind of ecosystem. An ecosystem may develop through various successions dependent on certain conditions. The conditions we have looked at here are mentioned in points 1–15 above. Given these conditions, it is highly probable that the 'ecosystem' will develop as an emergent,[3] where da Vinci organizational structures emerge without them being formally planned.

Rule-breaking organizations create da Vinci organizational structures, which continuously develop temporary disturbances. In other words, innovations are the temporary disturbances that continuously try to analogously knock the 'tight rope walker' off balance. The paradox is that the tight rope walker can only remain 'stable' on the rope by constantly moving his/her arms and legs. In rule-breaking organizations, innovations emerge precisely due to continuous temporary disruptions.

Rule-breaking organizations that achieve success in the global knowledge economy are very similar to what Normann terms 'prime movers':

> For the companies and other institutions which are able to organize value creation beyond their own boundaries, thereby setting the rules for others by effectively creating not only new products and services but shaping a new business context (what I will term ecogenesis) I reserve the term Prime Movers. (2004: 25)

In the same way as 'prime movers' change the infrastructure in larger systems (Normann, 2004: 83), da Vinci organizational structures change the social ecology in organizations. In some contexts, da Vinci organizational structures are a prerequisite for 'prime movers', while in other contexts, da Vinci organizational structures are created by 'prime movers'.

At the level of the individual, the way in which rule-breakers work may be compared to how artists work. They have the beginnings of an idea, that is, an undeveloped idea. In this phase, it is easy to quash the developing idea, because the rule-breakers are not even sure themselves how the idea will unfold, or the consequences of the idea. In this context, it is important to integrate into da Vinci organizational structures the principle that under no circumstances should it be allowed to quash ideas that are under development. In other words, in the initial stages of idea development there should be no critical input.

If one views idea development as a process that follows the path: beginnings of idea development, pre-concept, concept, and design, then it is only during the concept development phase that the critics or so-called 'devil's advocates' should be given a voice. Regarding the beginnings of idea development, and the pre-concept phase, only positive feedback should be given, because it is all too easy to quash an undeveloped idea. Metaphorically, the undeveloped idea and the pre-concept stage may be likened to the speechless baby, who needs help in order to learn how to talk. Figuratively, it is only in the concept and design phase that the child has acquired a simple language; so even in this phase, the 'devil's advocates' should act less like 'devils' and more like mentors. In other words, it is 'Socratic midwife' that will assist in the idea development. During the pilot and testing in a market, it is the details, and the notion that the idea should lead to an invoice that are given emphasis.

We have illustrated the above description in Fig. 3.8.

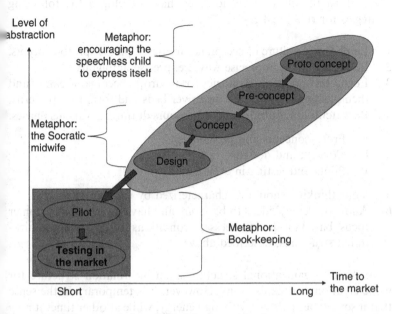

Figure 3.8 Process metaphors in da Vinci organization.

In order for the da Vinci organizational structures to unfold throughout the organization, it will be necessary for the leadership to protect the 'speechless babies' (i.e., developing ideas). We call such leaders da Vinci leaders for want of a better term. Da Vinci leaders base their thinking on positive psychology and positive leadership (Boniwell & Turagriu, 2019).

Developing concepts are woven into the organizational structure, in analogy with David Bohm's (2002) concept of 'implicate order', where threads are woven into established structures and then become the pattern that binds the entire organizational structure together. When this occurs, something emergent will also appear in the organization. This is not an externalization nor an internalization process, because at this point there is nothing to externalize or internalize. It is the unfinished, the imperfect, and the developing idea that slowly emerges through 'Socratic midwifery' dialogue. However, during this dialogue one should avoid making the mistake that one is controlling the birth of the concept. If one commits this error, the Socratic midwifery phase can easily become a conservative and overbearing process, thus inhibiting the development of da Vinci organizational structures.

Based on the above reflections, we have developed the following strategies for rule-breakers:

1 Emphasize a culture of acceptance for developing or proto-concepts.
2 Be precise in an imprecise way, i.e. precise ambiguity.
3 Focus on 'raindrop strategies': rain drops become streams, and then gushing rivers create new river beds and form new patterns.
4 Be watchful of attitudes and behaviours during the various phases:

   a Proto-concepts and pre-concepts.
   b Concept and design.
   c Pilots and testing in a market.

5 Your thinking should be characterized by win-win ideas.
6 Allow the 'crazy' ideas to blossom, and have an extreme customer focus, based on the 15 necessary conditions for da Vinci organizational structures, described above.

A da Vinci organizational structure is an information structure for value creation in organizations. However, it is temporary in the sense that it sometimes pulsates with high energy, while at other times it may almost go into hibernation. It is thus not temporary in the same way as projects are temporary, but temporary in the same way lightning and thunder are temporary natural phenomena. However, da Vinci organizational structures can evolve from being temporary and pulsating to becoming a permanent stable structures.

It should be emphasized that the da Vinci leader need not necessarily have a formal leadership role in an organization. The da Vinci leader may be attached to a formal leadership position, but he/she does not have to be. The da Vinci leader is the one who sees a need and takes leadership in relation to this need. For instance, one need not be a formal leader in an organization to act in relation to a need that emerges in a market or a potential market. The da Vinci leader takes leadership by utilizing resources in order to create value for the organization. In such situations, the formal leader's task will be to facilitate workable conditions for the functioning of this type of leadership, and the development of da Vinci organizational structures that can act in relation to meeting this need. The function of the da Vinci leader is to continuously expand the boundaries of the social system.

The da Vinci leader creates da Vinci organizational structures inside and outside the organization by connecting closely to the system of suppliers of products and services, their subcontractors, as well as consumers. This has been described by Toffler as the 'prosumer concept' (1980).

What is new is the pattern of interaction, where dynamic partnerships pulsate like a fusion energy and where the fuel of this energy is the temporary da Vinci organizational structures inside and outside the organization. The individual components of this fuel consist of the da Vinci leaders, the system of suppliers, and consumers. Da Vinci organizational structures are loosely linked to the established structure of the organization. Da Vinci organizational structures are temporary and may have a short lifespan, but can flare up again when new needs arise, and a new or former da Vinci leader sees the needs and acts in relation to them.

The formal leader should provide the da Vinci leader with an adequate room for manoeuvre and action outside established rules and procedures. The temporary aspect of da Vinci leadership does not necessarily mean that it will be of a short duration – it just means that da Vinci organizational structures exist as long as they result in extraordinary value creation. The temporary da Vinci organizational structures often have relationships with temporary da Vinci organizational structures in other organizations. The da Vinci relationships within the individual organization are strongly connected, while the relationships with da Vinci organizational structures in other organizations can be of varying strengths. Relationships with the established structures within the organization are loosely connected. The network that arises from these relationships is what we term 'dynamic partnership'. We have illustrated the above description in Fig. 3.9

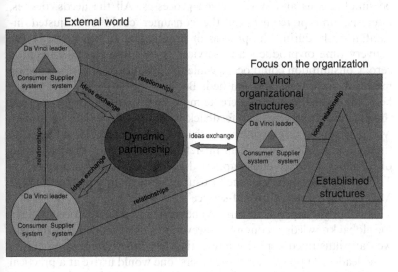

Figure 3.9 Da Vinci organizational structures within and between organizations.

The relationships lead to an exchange of ideas between the various da Vinci organizational structures within and between the organizations. This in turn creates the basis for dynamic partnerships. The da Vinci organizational structures are loosely linked to the existing structure of the organization in which they are located. Metaphorically, these loose connections enable serially connected explosions to occur regarding an organization's value creation performance. Normann (2004: 95) expresses this as follows: "The driving forces influencing value creation in the new economy explode and cascade our options to have co-production".[4]

It is the cascades of ideas exchanged between the da Vinci organizational structures that are crucial for value creation. However, it is the relationships that are the essential foundation. Therefore, knowledge of these relationships is important, or more abstractly, knowledge of the system of relationships that creates the supply of new 'fuel'. This knowledge can increase the life of da Vinci organizational structures within organizations.

While relationships may be considered the fuel of da Vinci organizational structures, the driving engine can be understood as the creative co-creation that takes place throughout the field, between da Vinci leaders, the system of suppliers, and the consumers.

Let us carry out the following thought experiment: If everything we consume was produced while we consumed it, then what would happen? One result would be that consumption and production would be simultaneous and synchronized processes. All the needs, desires, interests, and preferences of the consumer could be adjusted instantaneously during the process of production. In other words, the delivery time of products and services in this thought experiment is zero. Consumption could occur while the product or service was being modified, improved, and finished. Because the distribution time has been eliminated, this would create more time to qualitatively improve the product or service. The feedback would be immediate, and there would never be any problems with exceeding threshold values. The thought experiment may seem far-fetched; however, a similar system of production and consumption has already been proposed by Toffler's (1980) concept of the 'prosumer system', and by Gershuny & Miles' (1983) concept of 'self-service'.

The thought experiment can also be related to a modularized logic in the global knowledge economy, however, in a more moderate form than we have illustrated here. By integrating in a closely linked system da Vinci leaders, suppliers, and consumers, one would arrive at a practical variation of the thought experiment. In da Vinci organizational structures, the consumer can utilize the time gained to contribute to shaping the development of the product or service. Consumer feedback to da Vinci leaders and the system of suppliers would thus be instantaneous. In such a situation, the boundaries between producer and consumer would slowly disappear, and the possibility of tailor-made products and services would become a reality. If we like Normann (2004), replace the words consumer and customer with participator, co-creator, co-producer, and value creator, this will provide us with a new understanding of the meanings commonly associated with the words consumer and customer. In other words, value creation will take place in the interaction; that is, da Vinci organizational structures will facilitate value interaction. The core of the thought experiment is that one produces while consuming. The theoretical result can be expressed as value interaction and consumption as production. In practical terms, this will involve establishing closely knit relationships within da Vinci organizational structures. If many da Vinci organizational fields are allowed to freely unfold in the various organizations, this will result in a value-creating innovation system.

We have concretized the thought experiment in Fig. 3.10, which represents a model for co-creation in da Vinci organizational structures.

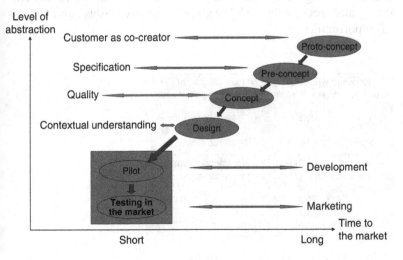

Figure 3.10 Value interaction.

The greater the degree of value interaction that takes place in da Vinci organizational fields, the greater will be the insight gained by the organization, and specifically the da Vinci leader, regarding the needs, wishes, interests, and preferences of customers.

Ideally, every customer should be involved in the entire sequence shown in Fig. 3.10 above, which is of course impossible in practice. However, if one assumes that consumption can be equated with production, then da Vinci leaders will gain insight into the needs, wishes, interests, and preferences of customers. Yet, something more than this would also become visible. The da Vinci leaders would gain insight into:

1   The customers' needs, wishes, interests, and preferences.
2   What customers do not need, do not want, are not interested in, and what are not their preferences.
3   What one does not know about the customers' needs, wishes, interests, and preferences,
4   What one does not know about what the customer does not want.

If one can gain knowledge of the four distinct knowledge domains, represented in points 1–4 above, then the value interaction will lead to improved efficiency, specialization, less resource wastage, and a greater room of opportunity for organizations. The value interaction window is shown in Fig. 3.11. This window can be helpful in promoting efficiency and specialization while reducing resource wastage and the loss of opportunities.

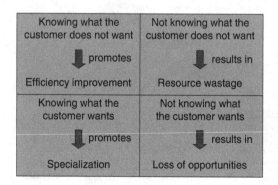

Figure 3.11 The value interaction window.

One of the critical success factors for da Vinci organizational structures is to encourage talented people who often work alone to participate in high-performance teams. We will focus on this in the next section.

Drawing maps that change the landscape

Da Vinci organizational structures in organizations can be found among individuals and teams that perform well. To further improve the performance of these individuals and teams, and those at the level below will enable the development of a creative field of innovation in the organization. However, using resources to improve the performance of mediocre and poorly performing groups is not the way to go (Gratton, 2007). In other words, we need to spread success not mediocrity.

There are several ways creative impulses can be spread throughout an organization. One can ask oneself the following questions: When I see a need, do I take the initiative to do something about it? How do I involve others and make partnerships so we can address the need together? To what extent do I take the initiative to work with others across organizational 'silos'? Gratton (2007: 173) says the following about the phenomenon we are trying to address here: "Hot spots emerge as a consequence of an interrelated system of practice and processes, behaviours and competencies".

There are three critical factors that emerge from the above description:

1   Initiatives and processes across established structures are a necessary prerequisite for creating and disseminating creative impulses.
2   Complementary skills that work together across organizational 'silos' provide opportunities for innovation.
3   The connections of various kinds across the functional areas of an organization create the conditions for creative fields of innovation.

In order to be able to spread creative energy fields in an organization, one should first identify where in the organization they already exist. For instance, there may be individuals in the various departments that have the necessary creativity to generate creative energy fields. This could be two people working in the same department, or two or more people working together across departments and functional areas. There may be teams in a department or teams in several departments.

There may be individuals and teams that have come together to solve a particular problem, or to study a specific challenge. These individuals, loosely structured groups or high-performing teams create creative impulses; it is these creative impulses one should attempt to generate and spread in the organization. These individuals and groups have one thing in common: they change very quickly in relation to changes in the market. They have sharp customer insight and as Annunzio (2004: 1) expresses, "they know how to get the internal resources they need to accomplish their goals". Consequently, the first step is to identify where in the organization these creative impulses exist. (Fig. 3.12)

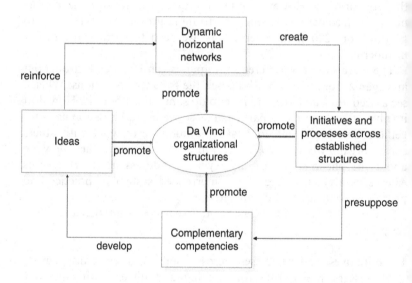

Figure 3.12 How da Vinci organizational structures emerge and develop.

Uncovering where in the organization these creative impulses exist will in practice involve finding out:

1   Who is collaborating with whom and with what results.
2   Where in the organization they are located.
3   Which networks they are part of.

Discovering the creative landscape in an organization, and then drawing a map of this landscape, means gaining insight into the origins and development of da Vinci organizational structures within organizations. Once this has been done, the next step is to identify intervention points.

The intervention points function as a compass that you will need to spread the creative impulses to other parts of the organization. The intervention points may be understood in relation to at least two levels:

1   Leadership level: What can and should the leadership do to spread creative impulses in an organization?
2   Individual level: What can individuals do to spread creative impulses in the organization?

Once you have determined the points of intervention, that is, when your compass has been set, then the final phase is to start finding your way 'across the terrain of the landscape', that is, what actions you should carry out. At a simplified level, the following figure can give an indication of the points of intervention and action strategies for developing and disseminating da Vinci organizational structures in organizations.

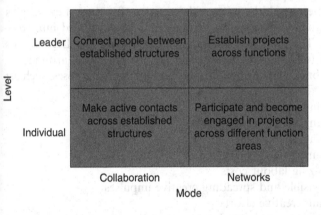

Figure 3.13 Points of intervention and action strategies for developing and disseminating da Vinci organizational structures in organizations.

A significant aspect of this approach is to be aware of the fact that 'the road is created as you go forward', because the terrain changes when people establish new networks and enter into new collaborative constellations.

If employees and the leadership actively use the creative innovation fields that exist in the established da Vinci organizational structures within the organization, then the performance of the entire organization will be improved (Annunzio, 2004: 1).

Envisioning an organization as being structured into a series of Lego bricks can enable a strategy for dissolving established and frozen structures. Using this strategy, the Lego bricks can simply be moved around and connected in order to spread creative energy. Some of the Lego bricks in the organization will be more vibrantly creative than others. Further, one can give the Lego bricks names depending on where they are located in the organization, and also colour them according to their degree of creative energy. The Lego bricks that have the greatest creative energy can be coloured red, representing 'hot'. The Lego bricks that have the least energy can be coloured blue 'frozen'. One can further imagine that one has varying shades of colours between the blue and the red, depending on the level of creative energy. For instance, a simple division could be the following: Red (hot), pink (relatively warm), purple (cool), and blue (frozen). When all the Lego bricks are literally spread out 'across the table', you will have a picture of how strongly the creative pulse beats in the organization at different locations, as well as where the creative pulse does not beat so strongly.

The next step would be to provide resources for those Lego bricks that are relatively warm (pink), so they may be developed into 'red' Lego bricks. The map that has now emerged using the Lego bricks may be used to change the terrain and not the other way around.

This Lego brick map method may be used for many purposes, such as:

- Developing productivity
- Developing better service quality
- Developing innovations
- Restructuring an organization
- Rationalizing labour costs
- Making visible and spreading creative impulses
- Rewarding creative efforts
- Implementing new strategies.

According to Annunzio's research (2004), the 'hot' areas in an organization (the red Lego bricks) possess the same characteristics in all the countries he has studied.[5] However, it should be noted that his research only focused on knowledge workers. He found three factors that were similar in all the countries he examined for top-performing working groups; they:

1   Respected and valued other people.
2   Promoted critical thinking.
3   Were always on the lookout for new opportunities.

It is important for organizations to create as many red Lego bricks as possible. For instance, they can do this by applying the three factors mentioned above, and focusing mainly on those Lego bricks that have the greatest potential to be red. An interesting and unexpected finding in Annunzio's international survey of knowledge workers' perfor- mance was that: "Only 10 percent of global knowledge workers,—, could provide evidence that their workgroup was high performing" (2004: 19). This finding suggests at least two things. Firstly, there is great potential for better leadership of knowledge workers. Secondly, there is a huge potential to create red Lego bricks in most organiza- tions. When more Lego bricks start to turn red, this will affect the behaviour of the whole organization.

Having a map that has the ability to change the terrain is ad- vantageous due to the fact that you acquire the power of definition and the power of determining which model should be used. The map also makes it possible to explore the Lego bricks, examining specifically what needs to be done to change behaviour to improve performance.

Based on the above description, we can now draw a map of the various Lego bricks in an organization. We have identified six main variables, which can cover the red, pink, purple, and blue Lego bricks. The red Lego bricks make up da Vinci's organizational structures within the organization. The six variables concern the degree of:

1 Appreciation and respect (1–9)
2 Critical thinking (1–9)
3 Opportunities available (1–9)
4 Cooperation (value - interaction) (1–9)
5 Horizontal networks (1–9)
6 Ideas' generation (1–9)

The highest level 7–9 correlates to the red Lego bricks; the scale 5–6 to pink; the scale of 3–4 to purple; and the scale of 1–2 to blue. Once a survey has been carried out in the organization in relation to the above we will have a picture of the various Lego bricks in the organization, how they are distributed, and what network they are a part of. Metaphorically, we may think of the survey as being created by a thermal imaging camera. Based on the survey, we can then draw a spider diagram of the various 'innovation temperatures' located in different places throughout the organization. Consequently, the spider diagram will provide a visualization of the number of Lego bricks and their various colours throughout the organization. The thermal imaging camera (the survey) provides an illustration of where the various innovation temperatures are 'geographically' located in the organization. The results of the survey and diagram will provide intervention points with regard to changing behaviour in the organization by starting with the red Lego bricks, and then focusing resources mainly on the pink Lego bricks, because these have the greatest potential to adopt da Vinci organizational structures, i.e. the ability to become red Lego bricks.

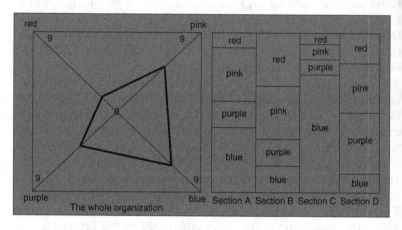

Figure 3.14 Innovation 'temperatures' in organizations.

Igniting the flame of innovation

The question we will consider in this section is: How can we ignite the flame of innovation in an organization? In the following, we will not focus on individual behaviour in organizations, but rather on collective behaviour and how it can be shaped, so that the innovation temperature makes the quantum leap we are looking for.

Surowiecki's research has shown that there are four factors that are important for making effective collective decisions: diversity, independence, decentralization, and coordination (2005). He presents us with a small account that shows something of the strength of his message: There are three groups: one group consists of 12 experts from a specific area in which a decision has to be made. The second group consists of 12 novices. The third group consists of 12 people who know nothing about the topic. Which of the groups will reach the correct decision? Of course, the answer is quite simple – the experts will in such a case almost always reach the right decision. However, a fourth group is introduced consisting of 4 experts, 4 novices, and 4 people who do not know anything about the specific topic or area. Who will get it right this time? Almost without exception it will be the composite group that gets it right. The reason is that under the right conditions composite groups often behave in a very effective manner, and are often 'smarter' than the non-composite groups consisting only of experts, says Surowiecki (2005: xiii). This can be explained by the fact that composite groups have a diversity of perspectives, and can think outside established mental models.

Earls' (2007) research of how mass behaviour can be changed shows that four factors are crucial: interaction, influence, connections, and co-creation. Relating Surowiecki's (2005) and Earls' research with Schelling's (1978) concept of micro-motives and macro-behavior, what we here term 'flocking', can provide us with some ideas of how the flame of innovation can be ignited in organizations. This is shown figuratively in Fig. 3.15.

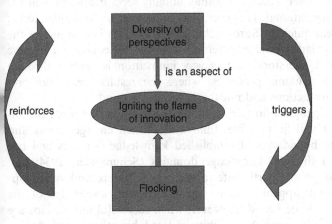

Figure 3.15 Igniting the flame of innovation in an organization.

Diversity of perspectives

Letting the 'thousands of flowers bloom' can often be just as effective for stimulating innovation as nourishing, and cultivating some 'selected flowers'. However, in an organizational context, the prerequisite is that you have the appropriate organizational structures that can facilitate the nourishment and cultivation of the thousands of flowers (Malhotra, 2020).

When everyone is given the opportunity to develop something new and creative, results will often be better than if you decide to bet on a single winner, because emerging innovations can rarely be identified within a well-defined problem area, but often show up as 'spin offs' in other problem areas than was initially imagined. This is supported by Hamel's (2000) Law of Innovation, which expresses that only two per thousand of emerging ideas will be dynamic enough to achieve market success. Consequently, when the aim is to develop an innovative idea, diversity is the key, because one can rarely know in advance what will be a market winner. In order to arrive at a satisfactory result, it is therefore advantageous to ensure that there is large diversity and to encourage the development of a large number of ideas (Balague & Elmoukhliss, 2021).

In other words, one does not know in advance which ideas will succeed. Knowledge always comes later, which is illustrated by the myth of the Owl of Minerva.[6] Therefore, as many people as possible should be encouraged to participate in the innovation process in order to create viable ideas, even if this may seem irrational and a waste of resources; in other words, what may initially seem irrational is in the long run very rational. However, it is important to 'recognize losers and kill them quickly' (Surowiecki, 2005: 29). This is also one of the main points made by Schumpeter in relation to the concept of creative destruction. Understood in this way innovation is created through chaotic and dynamic processes, where the results create the pre-conditions for actions and not the other way around.

The more people who participate in this process, the more combinations that will be possible. Innovations often emerge across and between the boundaries of established knowledge domains and not within the individual knowledge domains (Schumpeter, 1934: 66). When many people participate in the process, more and varied opportunities will appear, because the background knowledge of the participants will be varied. However, when successful innovations are created, the ideas will be quickly imitated by others, and, consequently, the scope of opportunities will eventually be reduced. Thus, the creative pulse of the economy will be stimulated, although this may first seem to be a waste of resources, but which is in reality a necessary pre-condition for new value creation.

To prevent the da Vinci organizational structures from dying, it is important to make sure that as many Lego bricks as possible start to glow red. If this does not occur, and the red Lego bricks become fewer, value creation will decrease, and the organization may start getting rid of some of the Lego bricks in order to cut costs (Syed, 2019). The point is that all the colours in the rainbow are needed in order to constitute the rainbow, i.e., the prerequisite for value creation in an organization.

In order to achieve success in the global knowledge economy, organizations need to continually innovate (Balague & Elmoukhliss, 2021), therefore, it is critical for organizations that more and more of the Lego bricks turn red. However, diversity must exist in relation to the other colours of Lego bricks. If all the Lego bricks turn red, this will not only ignite the flame of innovation but 'burn down the whole organization', because creativity will turn into chaos. The Lego bricks of other colours are necessary so that the red Lego bricks, when igniting the flame of innovation, do not result in the organization 'overheating'.

It is the continuous challenge to established thinking, which makes it possible to maintain the dynamics of an organization. It is a case of finding the balance between diversity and interaction, which enables the creation of that which is new without 'throwing the baby out with the bath water' (Cheong, 2005; Syed, 2019).

Using a religious analogy, it is the continuous incarnations of creative destruction in the organization that will give birth to more and more red Lego bricks. An important point is to ensure that those who are successful are not 'promoted' to bureaucratic leadership positions, because this will turn the red Lego bricks cold, which can quickly freeze and turn the entire organization into an ice block. Clothing the da Vinci leaders with a bureaucratic leadership cloak would be like hanging a millstone around the red Lego bricks, and lowering them to the depths of the sea, where it is always four degrees Celsius. The red Lego bricks are like perennial plants in the sense that they will continue to flower again and again if given the right conditions.

The main sources of nourishment for producing and maintaining the red Lego bricks, which develop and disseminate innovations, are the following:

1 The continuous addition of **new perspectives**
2 The emphasis on **cognitive diversity**
3 The reduction of 'group-think' by providing active and **creative critics**
4 An ever-increasing **expansion of opportunities**
5 Focusing on the importance of **original thinking**

In many contexts, diversity needs to be imposed on creative groups (the red and pink Lego bricks), because there will be a psychological and sociological drive to keep so-called dissenters out of the group (Malhotra, 2020). In order to form suitable composite groups and teams that can develop da Vinci organizational structures, it is well to keep in mind what Surowiecki says, when he expresses that "the value of expertise is in many contexts, overrated" (2005: 32). Although experts are important in many fields, it is very doubtful that one should only focus on groups consisting of experts if the aim is to ignite the flame of innovation in an organization. On the other hand, cognitive diversity within a group can be the spark that ignites the flame of innovation.

In order to establish cognitive diversity that can lead to the best results in an innovation context, two conditions should be fulfilled:

1   We need to identify:

    a   Collective blindness
    b   Conformity pressure
    c   Group thinking

2   We need to make sure that the three factors above are reduced as far as possible.

Group thinking occurs because one is not looking for the blind spots that obviously exist, which can be seen by others outside the group. Collective blindness occurs because you do not see the blind spots, even if you are looking for them. Conformity pressure arises because one conforms with the group out of convenience. In other words, one avoids disagreeing with an 'expert in the field'.

One should make sure that critical thinking exists within the group, and that 'devil's advocates', and so on, are given the opportunity to join the group. Group thinking is reduced by collecting information from outside the group. Collective blindness is reduced by developing and using early warning systems, which can detect signals, 'cues', and so on. One approach to alleviate the pressure of conformity is to make sure that everyone in the group always has an ally, i.e. a peer in the group.

Flocking

Da Vinci leadership is largely about learning to deal with disruptions, i.e. breaches in stable structures, where changes and new elements that were not planned are brought in. To learn to live with disruptions is to learn to cope with change processes, turbulence, and a high degree of complexity. Learning to live with uncertainty, ambiguity, and chaotic change processes concerns learning to master the demands of the new technology, e.g. artificial intelligence, intelligent robots, and intelligent algorithms.

Systems that are continuously exposed to a large degree of turbulence and complexity can also be found in the natural world. For instance, consider a flock of birds moving across the sky in coordinated and synchronized formation. The flock operates as a holistic system. It oscillates, changes direction, and behaves as a single unit. There is no visible leader in such a flock who controls the development of the formation.

An important point of da Vinci leadership is to help develop the team or group one leads, metaphorically understood as a flock of birds. A flock of this type acts as a whole organism, while at the same time the members act as independent, creative, and innovative individuals.

The behaviour of the flock is governed by certain simple rules, where each bird relates to the birds that are closest. We can transpose this idea to da Vinci organizational structures by saying that it is basic values, such as respect, responsibility, and dignity that guide the 'flock'. These simple, and at the same time important values, can constitute the basic management or guiding principle of the 'flock'. These three simple core values transform the team or group into a self-organizing system.

This is chaos theory and complexity theory in practice, i.e. some simple basic rules that govern complex behaviour. What makes such a 'flock' act as a whole is immediate feedback regarding deviations from the basic values. The feedback comes from leaders, colleagues, customers, etc. The individual employee should be committed to the core values, and be able to adapt to the feedback in relation to these core values. The speed of flight of a flock of birds is so great that only immediate feedback and immediate adaptation will work. The same applies to social systems when the pace of change, turbulence, and complexity is great. This will also be the case in the Fourth Industrial Revolution where the global connections will be dense and the spread of information will occur almost instantaneously throughout the global system. The core values should therefore be simple and easy to understand, even if they have different levels of depth. It is the simple basic rules that govern complex behaviour not the other way around.

All living systems are dependent on feedback. Sometimes it has to be immediate, other times the feedback is delayed. In both cases, there will be certain threshold values that should not be exceeded. If this happens, irreversible processes can endanger the entire system.

Flocking is illustrated in Fig. 3.16.

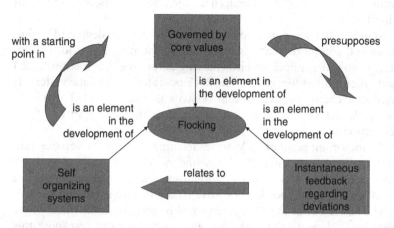

Figure 3.16 Flocking.

Self-organization is based on self-management. Self-management here means managing oneself, one's colleagues, competitors, customers, and suppliers. Self-management is also directly linked to developing the creativity or entrepreneurial spirit of the employees.

In order to succeed with self-organization, it will also be crucial to develop the flock's interaction competence, i.e. how the individual members of the 'flock' relate to each other. This concerns developing collaborative abilities and social and emotional competence.

As a general rule, it will be the interaction between the members of the group that ultimately triggers the flame of innovation, rarely external demands and instructions. When individuals interact with each other, a complex macro-behaviour is ultimately created in the system, says the Nobel Prize winner in economics Schelling (1978). Schelling's says that it is simple basic rules that can lead to complex behaviour in the larger social system, not unlike the seemingly complex behaviour of a flock of birds. According to Schelling, it is the simple basic rules that trigger the phenomenon of flocking. The 'flock' we are interested in here is the group or team that triggers the flame of innovation in an organization. Regarding the phenomenon of flocking (micro-motive), which triggers macro-behaviour, we are often confused by a mixture of what is complicated and what is complex (complexity). That something is complicated can mean that many individuals are interacting, and it is therefore difficult for the individual to understand exactly what is happening. That something is complex does not have to be triggered by the fact that many parts interact, but when they interact, something completely new arises that cannot be understood by analyzing the individual parts, and then putting them together into a whole. The new that emerges is what we term an emergent in relation to the individual parts.

In this context, this has been brought in to show that igniting the flame of innovation, which is a flocking phenomenon, triggers a large degree of complexity, because it is based on interaction between individuals. If we try to understand flocking as if it were caused by complicated behaviour, then we will have great difficulty in coming to terms with the phenomenon. The reasoning is simple. You simply cannot take the 'flock' apart to see what makes it tick. Flocking is based on complex behaviour, not complicated behaviour. The question that arises from this is the following: How can understanding the distinction between complicated behaviour and complex behaviour help us to understand the phenomenon – 'igniting the flame of innovation'? The answer is straightforward: We need to start with the whole, i.e. the group, and the activity the group is part of, in order to understand the behaviour of the individual members, not the other way around. It is not the micro-behaviour itself that is interesting, but how the macro-behaviour eventually manifests itself.

If, on the other hand, we take as our starting point that the phenomenon is complicated, then the focus will be on the individuals. However, the starting point in flocking is the whole, and how this whole interacts with the larger system of which it is a part.

The difference between complex and complicated behaviour should not be misunderstood to the point that simple basic rules do not mean anything for complexity. Simple basic rules are crucial to understanding complexity. The basic assumption of flocking is that simple basic rules trigger complexity when they interact with each other.

Flocking can take place both in expert groups and when the composition is based on what we term cognitive diversity. Igniting the flame of innovation, on the other hand, is linked to complexity and cognitive diversity. The simple structural principles of cognitive diversity are as follows:

1   Use external information, because this will reduce group thinking.
2   Integrate early warning signals, because this will reduce collective blindness.
3   Always have an ally within the group, as this will reduce conformity pressure.

The simple basic rules of behaviour are as follows:

1   Value and respect the other members of the group.
2   Promote critical thinking.
3   Always look for opportunities.

When the behaviour and actions of the group are based on simple basic rules, there are no plans or phases that need to be followed in order to eventually create innovations. On the other hand, 'the communities of purpose' (Kanter, 2006) should be very clear within the group. In other words, 'the communities of purpose' is what guides group behaviour.

What emerges on an abstract level is that random events or actions over time create a pattern (macro-behaviour) that promotes stability. However, the paradox is that stability presupposes change. If stability is not linked to change, rigidity can easily develop. A metaphor that is often used to explain this paradox is that of the tight rope walker. The tightrope walker has to constantly change the position of his/her arms and legs to remain 'stable' on the tightrope. Rigidity leads to social death, just as the tight rope walker would fall down if he kept his/her arms and legs completely still. In other words, change is not the opposite of stability, but rigidity. In this context, one way to ignite the flame of innovation in da Vinci organizational fields is to be very observant of what may seem like a random event. We have illustrated the above description in Fig. 3.17.

Schelling (1978) points out that the behaviour of individuals leads to emergents at the system level when simple basic rules control behaviour and actions. In other words, when a group has a common purpose ('community of purpose'), emergents can appear on another level. The 'purpose' is to ignite the flame of innovation, not to develop specific innovations, such as product or process innovations. These will eventually be developed through the pattern created in the group, once the innovation flame has been ignited.

A prerequisite for this to occur is that the purpose corresponds to people's intentions, because the intentions at the micro level will trigger the desired behaviour at the macro level. The greater the extent of the da Vinci organizational field within the organization, the less people's intentions need to be the same in order for the behaviour throughout the da Vinci organizational field to trigger the desired pattern, because there will be groups of individuals within the da Vinci organizational field who have the same intentions. When the purpose is clear, and there are simple basic rules that are followed, then there will always be someone who has intentions that correspond to the purpose. These people, no

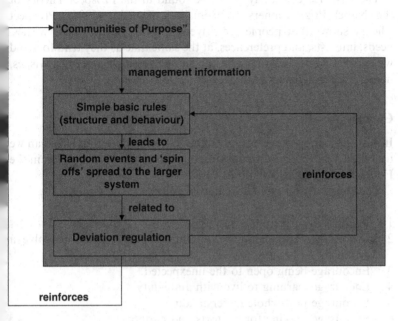

Figure 3.17 Micro strategies that ignite the flame of innovation and change macro-behaviour.

matter where they may be physically located, will seek to cooperate with each other to create the first spark that can ignite the flame of innovation, because they will seek to maximize success measured against a specific variable. For the organization as a whole, it is not of interest which of the actors or which of the groups achieve success, and which do not. However, for the individual or the group, success can be a matter of being 'seen', and thus linked to resource allocation. For the organization it is only important that someone succeeds, not who succeeds. Success, in this context, is to ignite the flame of innovation.

An implication from a business perspective is that you first look at the results achieved, and then you allocate resources. First results and then planning, not the other way around, is a principle in flocking. In this context, the so-called Matthew effect, 'He who has will be given more' can be rewritten as, 'He who achieves more will be given more'. The reason is that such individuals and groups are those that ignite the flame of innovation, create da Vinci organizational fields, and increase value creation through the creation of innovations, which thus lifts up the entire organization.

The basis for this analysis can be found in the Prospect Theory of the Nobel Prize winners Kahneman & Tversky (1984). Prospect Theory shows that people are driven by what satisfies their wishes, needs, interests, and preferences, at the same time as they tend to avoid what in the short or long term can harm their own interests, wishes, needs, and preferences (Adriaenssen & Johannessen, 2016).

Conclusion

In this chapter, we have examined the following question: How can we utilize da Vinci organizational structures to promote innovation in the Fourth Industrial Revolution?

The short answer can be written as follows:

1 Encourage curiosity.
2 Encourage experimenting with different approaches to solve a problem.
3 Encourage being open to the unexpected.
4 Encourage learning to live with ambiguity.
5 Encourage part-whole understanding.
6 Encourage looking for contexts and patterns.

The six points above can be summarized by saying that in order for da Vinci methodology to be developed, an environment should be encouraged where the original and new can grow and flourish. A simple micro-strategy to promote this development is to curb conformist thinking while rewarding original thinking.

Notes

1 See: Chesbrough, 2006; Taylor & LaBarre, 2007: 64–87; DiBona et al., 1999, Syed, 2019.
2 Regarding the figure, we have termed points 1, 2, 4, 5, 14, and 15 value creation for customers; points 3, 7, and 11 are termed 'genuine customer experience'. Point 6 is termed 'creative conceptual destruction'. We have termed points 7, 11, and 13 open and 'crowd' innovation models. Points 8 and 9 are explained within the text.
3 By emergent we mean: 'Let S be a system with composition A, i.e. the various components in addition to the way they are composed. If P is a property of S, P is emergent with regard to A, if and only if no components in A possess P; otherwise P is to be regarded as a resulting property with regards to A' (Bunge, 1977:97).
4 'Hot spots' (Gratton, 2007), 'Mavericks' (Taylor & Labarre (2007), and creative energy fields in organizations.

5 USA, Europe (France, Italy, the Netherlands, Sweden, England), Japan, Australia, China, (Peking, Shanghai).
6 https://en.wikipedia.org/wiki/Owl_of_Athena

References

Adriaenssen, D and J-A Johannessen. "Conceptual Generalization: Methodological Reflections. A Systemic viewpoint." *Kybernetes*, 44, no. 4(2015): 588–605.
Adriaenssen, J-A and J-A Johannessen. "Prospect Theory as an Explanation for Resistance to organizational Change: Some Management Implications." *Problems and Perspectives in Management*, 14, no. 2 (2016): 84–92.
Annunzio, SL. *Contagious Success*. New York: Portfolio, 2004.
Balague, C and M Elmoukliss. *From Open to Crowd Innovation*. London: ISTE, 2021.
Beer, S. *Diagnosing the System for Organizing*. London: Wiley, 1985.
Bohm, D. *Wholeness and Implicate Order*. London: Routledge, 2002.
Boniwell, I and D Turagriu. *Positive psychology, Research and Applications*. London: Open University Press, 2019.
Bunge, M. *The Furniture of the World*. Dordrecht: Reidel, 1977.
Cheong, LY, C Juma, and JD Sachs. *Innovation: Applying Knowledge in Development*. New York: Earthscan Publications Ltd., 2005.
Chesbrough, H. *Open Business Models*. Boston: Harvard Business School Press, 2006.
Collins, JC. *Good to Great: Why Some Companies Make the Leap and Others Don't*. New York: Harper Business, 2001.
Collins, JC and JI Porras. *Built to Last*. New York: Collins, 1994.
Di Bona, C, S Ockman, and M Stone (Ed.). *Open Sources: Voices from the Open Source Revolution*. New York: O'Reilly Media, 1999.
Dong, L, Y Gong, J Zhou, and J-C Huang. "Human Resource Systems, Employee Creativity, and Firm Innovation: The Moderating Role of Firm Ownership." *Academy of Management Review*, 60, no. 3 (2017): 1164–1188.
Earls, M. *Welcome to the Creative Age*. New York: John Wiley, 2007.
Farrell, W. *How Hits Happen*. New York: Harper Collins, 1998.
Gershuny, J and I Miles. *The New Service Economy: The Transformation of Employment in Industrial Societies*. London: Frances Pinter, 1983.
Gratton, L. *Hot Spot*. London: Prentice Hall, 2007.
Hamel, G. *Leading the Revolution*. Boston: Harvard Business School Press, 2000.
Hamel, G. *The Management of the Future*. Boston: Harvard Business School Press, 2007.
Hansen, MT. "The Search Transfer problem: The Role of Weak ties in sharing Knowledge across organizational Subunits." *Administrative Science Quarterly*, 44 (1999): 82–111.

Johannessen, J-A. *The Workplace of the Future: The Fourth Industrial Revolution, the precariat and the Death of Hierarchies.* London: Routledge, 2018.

Johannessen, J-A. *Automation, Capitalism and the End of the Middle Class.* London: Routledge, 2019.

Johannessen, J-A. *Historical Introduction to Knowledge Management and the Innovation Economy.* London: Emerald, 2019a.

Johannessen, J-A. *Building the Innovation Economy.* London: Emerald, 2020. Routledge, London.

Johannessen, J-A. *Ethics, Innovation, and Artificial Intelligence: Challenges in the Fourth Industrial Revolution.* London: Routledge, 2021.

Johannessen, J-A. *The Fourth Industrial Revolution and Competence,* London: Routledge, 2022.

Johannessen, J-A and H Sætersdal. *Automation, Innovation and Work: The Singularity Innovation,* 2020.

Kahneman, D and A Tversky. "Choices, values and Frames." *American Psychologist,* 39, no. 4 (1984): 341–350.

Kanter, RM. "From Cells to communities: Deconstructing the Organization." In *Organization Development,* edited by, JV Gallos, 858–888. San Francisco: Jossey Bass, 2006.

Kim, WC and R Mauborgne. *Blue Ocean Strategy.* Boston MA: Harvard Business School Press, 2005.

Liker, JK. *The Toyota Way.* New York: McGraw-Hill, 2004.

Luhmann, N. *Social Systems.* Stanford: Stanford University Press, 1995.

Malhotra, A. *Unleashing the Crowd: Collaborative Solutions to Wicked Business and societal problems.* London: Palgrave, 2020.

Normann, R. *Reframing Business: When the Map Changes the Landscape.* New York: John Wiley & Sons, 2004.

Ramirez, R and J Wallin. *Prime Movers: Define Your Business or Have Someone Define It against You.* New York: John Wiley & Sons, 2000.

Schelling, T. *Micromotives and Macrobehavior.* London: W.W. Norton, 1978.

Schumpeter, JA. *The Theory of Economic Development.* Cambridge, MA: Harvard University Press, 1934.

Surowiecki, J. *The Wisdom of Crowds.* London: Doubleday, 2005.

Syed, M. *Rebel Ideas: The power of Diverse Thinking.* New York: John Murray, 2019.

Taylor, WC and PG LaBarre. *Mavericks at Work.* New York: William Morrow, 2007.

Toffler, A. *The Third Wave.* New York: Collins, 1980.

4 Da Vinci organization and innovation culture

Key points in this chapter

- Organizations are both complex and complicated at the same time.
- Self-organization is based on clear and basic rules.
- An emergent is something qualitatively new, which emerges in social systems, when we move from one level to the next.
- Following a few simple basic rules can lead to complex social behaviour.
- Synchronizing knowledge can result in spontaneous creative processes.

Introduction

The starting point for this chapter is that organizations are complex adaptable social systems. That something is complicated is not the same as that it is complex. When a system is complex we can say that it is composed of so many interconnected parts that it is basically impossible to have full knowledge of the consequences of the interactions between the parts.

If we say that something is complicated, this is often a subjective view. In other words, what may be perceived as complicated by one person may be perceived as simple by another.

Organizations are both complex and complicated at the same time. For instance, some people may have insight into the workings of one part of the organization, while others have insight into other parts, while no one has insight into everything that occurs within the organization.

If we view organizations as being complicated, then this often concerns the individual's level of knowledge in relation to what is occurring in the organization, where it is occurring, who is involved, and what is the effect. On the other hand, if we view an organization as

DOI: 10.4324/9781003335726-4

being a complex social system, then this concerns to a lesser extent the level of knowledge one has, but more a question of attitudes, i.e. what one thinks, says and does in different situations (Baker, 1995).

If we view organizations as being complex adaptable social systems, with one or more purposes, then we can not metaphorically, or in reality, take them apart to see how they work, and then put them back together again. You can only do this if you view organizations as complicated systems. However, viewing organizations as complicated systems does not mean that we will gain greater insight into the complexities of social systems. By taking this approach, we may feel that we think we know, because we view organizations as causal systems. So what does this have to do with the culture of experience transfer? The answer is straightforward. It has everything to do with culture and experience transfer, because how we think and communicate about and in social systems is precisely the core of both culture and experience transfer. It is our attitude towards complex adaptable social systems that constitutes the starting point of how we understand them. It is not what we think or how we view complex adaptable social systems that are central to developing a culture that promotes innovation and organizational entrepreneurship, but that we allow and encourage different ways of thinking (Cooper et al., 2016). In such a culture, the creative new will be able to unfold more easily and be used for the benefit of all stakeholders. It is the room of opportunity that increases when we allow everyone to think freely and act freely, given ethical limitations. As the room for opportunity increases, so does the probability of the innovative new emerging, because when different ways of thinking are connected, the probability of the creative new emerging increases (Chenowelth, 2020).

It is for this reason that it is crucial to distinguish between something that is complicated and something that is complex. If a social system such as an organization or business is complex, then it is not of much help to analyze the system in order to gain insight into how it works. This type of thinking may be compared to the idea of unfolding a circle into a straight line in order to explain that the circle has a beginning and an end. An essential point of a circle is that it has neither a beginning nor an end. If one views a circle as having a beginning and an end, then one is thinking linearly. Of course, there is nothing wrong in thinking linearly depending on the context and situation, but if the context is circular, then it would be erroneous to use linear thinking. In other words, one needs to take the context into consideration, and not mix circular contexts with linear contexts, if one wishes to avoid misunderstandings and erroneous conclusions.

Complexity theory concerns the study of complex systems (**not** complicated phenomena), such as organizations. It draws from research in various fields, such as the natural sciences, and is concerned with non-linearity rather than linear analysis (Brown & Eisenhardt, 2001). Complexity theory can also be used to describe emergent phenomena; expressed simply, in complex systems, 2 + 2 is not necessarily equal to 4. Emergents appear at a higher level within a system; the combination of properties at a lower level (2 + 2), cannot be used to predict an emergent that appears at a higher level (not 4). Expressed in another way, we cannot understand the whole by only examining the individual parts; when studying emergent phenomena, we need to study the whole (holistic approach rather than an atomic approach).

Complexity theories deal with both physical systems, biological systems, historical systems, sociological systems, cybernetic systems, and chaotic systems. Complexity theory is, like systems theory, not one single theory, but many different theories that are concerned with the same phenomena, i.e. emergent phenomena.[1]

Organizations are both complex and complicated. They are complicated in the sense that they can be administered, managed, and governed. They are complex in the sense that a culture that promotes purpose needs to be developed, and a culture cannot be managed and governed in a mechanistic sense. The culture needs to be co-created, self-organized, and can in a certain sense also be guided and managed.

The innovation culture in da Vinci organization is developed through the interaction between emergent phenomena, self-organization, and synchronization.

In this chapter, we will examine the following question: How can we utilize da Vinci's culture of innovation to promote innovation in the Fourth Industrial Revolution?

In order to answer this question, we have formulated three research questions:

RQ1 How can emergent phenomena contribute to the development of a culture of innovation in da Vinci organization?

RQ2 How can self-organization contribute to developing a culture of innovation in da Vinci organization?

RQ3 How can synchronization contribute to developing a culture of innovation in da Vinci organization?

We have illustrated the above description in Fig. 4.1. Fig. 4.1 also shows how this chapter is organized.

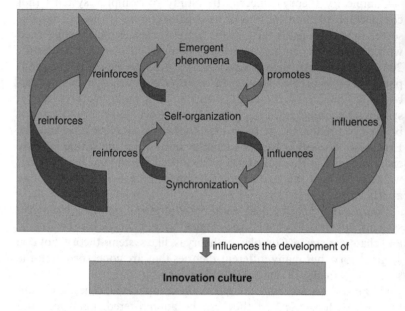

Figure 4.1 Da Vinci's culture of innovation.

Emergent phenomena

In this section, we will examine the following question: How can emergent phenomena contribute to the development of a culture of innovation in da Vinci organization?

An emergent is something qualitatively new, which emerges in social systems, when we move from one level to the next (Bunge, 1998: 73). The characteristics of the individuals in an organization do not tell us much about an organization's culture. The culture is emergent in relation to the level of the individual. Emergent phenomena also appear when we consider the whole and not the parts in social systems. The whole has emergent properties that the parts lack, says Bunge (1998: 72).

We view culture as being an emergent phenomenon in organizations. An organization's culture is created by the dynamic relationships within the organization, and how the organization's parts interact to create a whole. Systemic theory can help us to understand culture in relation to emergent phenomena.

Simplified, we can say that systemic thinking focuses on:

• 'Parts and whole' problems
• Relationships

- Processes
- Patterns
- Circular contexts
- Interaction

In systemic thinking, we are constantly searching for the pattern that binds phenomena together, or, as expressed by Bateson (1972: 155) 'the pattern which combines'. Dissecting a swallow tells us little about aerodynamic principles, but a swallow, viewed as a whole, has within it information that is complementary to aerodynamic principles. In the same way, the parts must always be classified 'according to the relations between them' (Bateson, 1972; 154).

Utilizing systemic theory, organizational culture is viewed as an emergent pattern, which connects the parts in such a way that it creates identity for the individual in the organization.

In order to understand emergent phenomena it can be useful to consider:

1 The larger whole the phenomenon is part of
2 The external world the phenomenon operates in
3 The parts that constitute the phenomenon
4 The individuals involved, to grasp the underlying attitudes and values of a system.

An emergent phenomenon cannot be fully understood, and requires a different approach than analysis with regards to understanding and explaining the phenomenon.

Emergent phenomena in social systems, such as an organization's culture, can influence the behaviour of its members. For instance, if the organization's culture is characterized to some extent by 'arrogance', then it will be highly probable that its members will exhibit a condescending attitude towards members of other organizations.

In this context, an organization's culture not only affects the behaviour of its members, but also their way of thinking, communicating, and acting, as well as how they perceive themselves in relation to the larger system they are part of.

It is difficult and perhaps impossible to control and monitor the development of emergent social phenomena. Complex problems in an organization can be solved when the members of the organization carry out their own activities, execute their roles, and focus on the results they are expected to achieve. Emergent social phenomena can be managed by redefining these elements. For instance, one can change an organization's culture by:

- Redefining roles
- Developing new activities and processes in the organization
- Establishing new relationships by reorganizing
- Creating other expectations by changing what is rewarded, etc.

However, the leadership needs to know which culture is desired and which culture is not desired. If, for example, you want an innovation culture, then there are other criteria that will be important, then if you want a performance culture. If you want both an innovation and performance culture, then certain organizational measures need to be taken that will promote both innovation and performance.

When we are examining emergent social phenomena, we need to look at different levels, and the parts and the whole, in addition to considering the contextual aspect. Contextual understanding is emergent in relation to part understanding, i.e. the whole has properties that we do not find by only examining the parts (Bunge, 1998: 72–73).

Understanding and explaining these emergent phenomena presupposes both a cross-disciplinary and an interdisciplinary approach. In an organizational culture, individuals constitute the lowest level. At the next level are the relationships between individuals. At the third level are the relationships between groups. In order not to complicate the picture, we stop at this level, and look at what steps can be taken to guide the development of an organizational culture indirectly.

At the individual level, as mentioned above, we can change expectations, role descriptions, activities, and processes. At the relational level, we can reorganize, re-group, and relocate in order to change the relationships between individuals. At the group level, we can communicate clear messages about the desired behaviour, as well as reward the desired behaviour. We will use a somewhat devised example just to make the point about how organizational groups can be structured in a completely different way: the management has informed employees when creating work groups that those groups consisting of 50% left-handed members will receive a 50% salary increase. In addition, the 'left-handed groups' will receive a 100% salary increase if they work together with other 'left-handed groups'. In other words, such an instruction from the management would result in a change in group compositions and the relations between groups.

We have illustrated how one can guide the development of an organization's culture indirectly in Fig. 4.2.

The point we have tried to convey is that an emergent social phenomenon can be managed and changed by indirect action at the

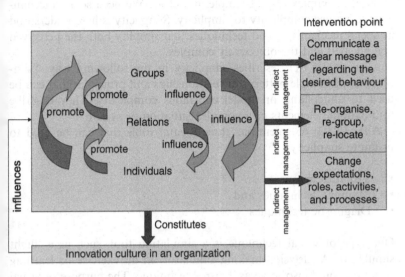

Figure 4.2 Guiding the development of an organization's culture indirectly.

levels below the emergent phenomenon. However, perhaps an explanation is needed for those readers who are used to viewing social systems as being comprised of three levels: micro, meso, and macro. Although social systems are usually viewed as consisting of three levels, some researchers may find it appropriate to view them as consisting of more than three levels. The point we are attempting to make here is that the various models of researchers consisting of three or more levels are abstractions, while emergent phenomena exist in the real world. In other words, it may hinder our understanding of a phenomenon, if we divide social systems into levels according to what is deemed appropriate. For instance, in addition to micro, meso, and macro, we may also include other levels, such as 'pico, nano, and giga' (Bunge, 1998: 73). The purpose of being aware of the many levels is to show that emergent phenomena can occur at different levels, not just at the meso and macro levels – although it may be appropriate to think in terms of micro, meso, and macro for pedagogical reasons.

The thinking here is that emergent phenomena are just as real as concrete phenomena, they are just more complex. In a world where emergent phenomena occur on many different levels, and where patterns emerge and change rapidly, the future will seem uncertain and chaotic. In such a culture, it will be greatly advantageous if we can make the complex appear simple and clear. We need social mechanisms to reduce complexity to simplicity. Simplicity is here understood as social mechanisms and techniques that simplify both the perceived complicated and the objectively complex.

Allee (2003: 61) describes simplicity in the following way: "simplexities are simple patterns of relationships and principles that can be used to understand or model enormous complexity. They describe foundational elements of a complex situation or system".

Allee (2003: 65) mentions three mental tools that can be used to promote simplicity:

- Visual techniques
- Mapping techniques and
- Diagnostic techniques

One type of visual technique is a simulation tool, such as a 'flight simulator'. A 'decision-making simulator' in an exercise or learning situation could also serve as a visual technique. The purpose of visual techniques is, amongst other things, to enable communication that can help a group in real decision-making situations, as well as to identify situations that, in real situations, could have been costly if they were learnt from practice.

'Games' are an example of a 'mapping' technique. For instance, Klein (2003) shows in his study how the US Army use 'decision games' to develop intuitive skills. Another 'mapping' technique can be the visualizing of a business process. This can be done with various model-building tools using artificial intelligence, intelligent robots, and intelligent algorithms. Toyota's visualization technology for control functions is a practical and easy way to do this (Liker, 2004: 303). The simplest 'mapping' techniques are perhaps flow charts and organization charts.

There are many creative tools described in the literature (Gelb, 2004) which can be termed 'diagnostic techniques' for unleashing creativity in groups. We can find other diagnostic techniques, among others, in Beer (1985), who through his VSM model (Viable System Model) diagnoses organizations as five different but integrated systems. Miller (1978) has also developed diagnostic methods for 20 critical subsystems in organizations.

The purpose of 'simplexities', according to Allee, is to: "work more effectively in the complex world" (2003: 66). Simple basic rules can, through self-organization, make it possible to operate the most complex systems. Air traffic, road traffic, bees collecting nectar, etc. are all examples of how simple basic rules make it possible to relate to a large degree of complexity.

In the economic subsystem, there are simple basic rules for determining prices and the relationship between supply and demand. In social subsystems, one can imagine that simple basic rules could be used in relation to standards of respect, responsibility, and dignity. The point here is that 'simplexities' can maintain large complex social systems.

We have designed a simplexity matrix in Fig. 4.3. The matrix consists of three layers. The outer layer is the operative one. The middle layer is the empirical one, i.e. where the operative is practiced. The innermost layer is the conceptual one, where the conceptual generalizations take place. The outer layer consists of rules, procedures, systematizations, functions, coordination, and integration. The middle layer consists of structure, codes (methods), targets (target groups), purpose, results (frameworks), and evaluation. The innermost layer consists of data, information, knowledge, meaning, reflection, and insight (wisdom). The core in the middle is thought to be where the emergent occurs. In order to understand the nature of emergents in

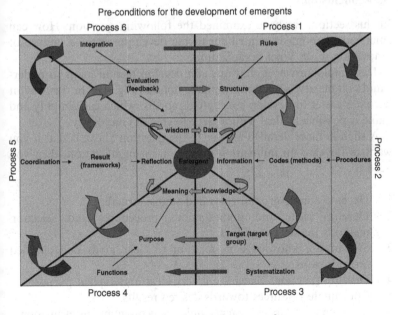

Figure 4.3 The pre-conditions for the development of emergents.

relation to this matrix, one should have an understanding of the functioning of the three layers and the adjacent six processes.

In the individual main parts of the matrix, the following six processes take place:

1   Rules that structure data
2   Procedures that through understanding codes create information
3   Systematization towards one or more goals, which creates knowledge
4   Functions that have a purpose and thus create meaning
5   Coordination towards results, which develops reflection
6   Integration through evaluation that creates insight (wisdom)

The purpose of Fig. 4.3 is to show a visualization of some of the basic processes in any social system at an abstract level, in analogy with analytical models, which can function as mental maps for the emergence of emergents. Each of the six processes in the three layers of Fig. 4.3 can be understood separately, and they can also be understood in context, i.e. in relation to each other.

Sub-conclusion

In this section, we have examined the following question: How can emergent phenomena contribute to the development of a culture of innovation in da Vinci organization?

The simple answer is that one can develop mental maps to understand complexity, something we have done in Fig. 4.3. In this way, it becomes easier to develop conceptual models, which can simplify and make it possible to deal with a large degree of complexity.

A slightly more detailed answer to the question above is that if you want to develop an innovation culture in an organization, then you need to:

1   Develop simple ground rules and simple structures.
2   Develop clear and unambiguous procedures and selection methods for selecting ideas.
3   Systematize knowledge in relation to clear goals and clarified target groups.
4   Develop functions that have a very clear and explicit purpose.
5   Coordinate resources towards desired results.
6   Integrate all feedback systems and conduct continuous evaluations.

Self-organization

In this section, we will examine the following question: How can self-organization contribute to developing a culture of innovation in da Vinci organization?

Self-organization seems to arise in most complex social systems (Balague & Elmoukliss, 2021). Self-organization can be described as emergent behaviour in such systems. Self-organization seems to arise as a spontaneous pattern formation when several subsystems interact with each other. As we argued when discussing emergents, complex social behaviour can result from following a few simple basic rules. A good deal of research in chaos and complexity theory indicates a basic pattern of self-organization in socially adaptive complex systems.[2] On a general level, the pattern can be described as follows: a. 'Tip', 'turn', 'setback'; b. 'Tip', 'turn', 'progress', and then back to a. 'Tip' stands for 'tipping point', or the point signifying that a critical threshold has been reached after which the system shifts radically into a different state. Turn stands for 'turning point' – the point when the change occurs. Setbacks and progress can be both the subjectively experienced, as well as the objective i.e. testable results of setbacks and progress. Between turning point and tipping point, there seems to be a period of long hard work (LHW) that can be experienced by many as not leading anywhere. However, if the 'long hard work' is not executed, then nothing happens, or in terms of pattern understanding, it will take a very long time before the tipping point occurs. We cannot know in advance which event, small or large, will cause tipping points to occur. This may be a completely random and personally experienced insignificant occurrence that makes the 'cup overflow'. However, this insignificant occurrence can become very significant in its social consequences, because it triggers a tipping point, and then irreversible accelerating processes are set in motion. Self-organization can be understood as the period between tipping point and turning point.

We have illustrated this pattern in Fig. 4.4.

There is much to suggest that it is in the tip-turn phase that innovations either drive the phase or are driven by the phase. In the tip-turn phase, self-organization occurs as spontaneous behaviour, in analogy with the movements of a bird flock and the formation of patterns. It is the micro-behaviour that seems to create the macro-structures, in analogy to the fact that it is the small deviations that the individual bird makes in a flock of birds that creates the pattern we see in the movements of a flock of birds (Schweitzer, 1997). The

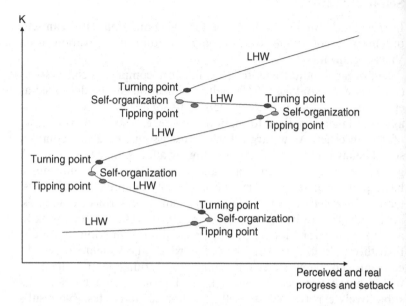

Figure 4.4 Generic patterns in adaptive complex social system: Tip-turn set-back; Tip turn progress.[3]

micro-movement is governed by a certain rules, e.g. some simple deviation rules, which can be of the form: If the behaviour of the next actor (bird, fish, etc.) becomes greater than x, then correct the distance so that the distance is not greater than x. If all the actors are governed by such simple deviation rules, then the macrostructure will form a holistic pattern. An external observer may easily imagine the pattern as if it is controlled by an overriding will, a leader who controls it all. In reality, it is a case of following some simple basic rules that are the guiding principle for the whole pattern.

The various rules for micro-behaviour will be adapted to the local context. The point here is that the local rules and routines in an organization will provide guidance for the behaviour that the system exhibits as a whole. The consequence of this for the leadership is that if one is to control a culture, which is an emerging macro phenomenon, then one should define some very explicit basic rules at the local level for the actors in the system.

The local basic rules in a complex system, such as an organization operating in a competitive market, will be dependent on two overriding factors (Schweitzer & Zimmermann, 2001: 277):

1   The actors should have a room of opportunity, i.e. they should have choices.
2   There should be a room of opportunity for relationships between the actors, i.e. real possibilities for constructive relations between the actors.

Patterns and self-organization will also depend on how the external world places restrictions on the system. In analogy with a school of fish, one could imagine that the general basic rules are:

•   Avoid danger
•   Keep distance x plus minus y to the next individual.[4]

Regarding Fig. 4.5, the implications for the leadership's guidance of an organizational culture, and the points of intervention will be:

1   Adopt a few clear, simple basic rules.
2   Examine and possibly change the room of opportunity for the actors and for the relations between the actors.

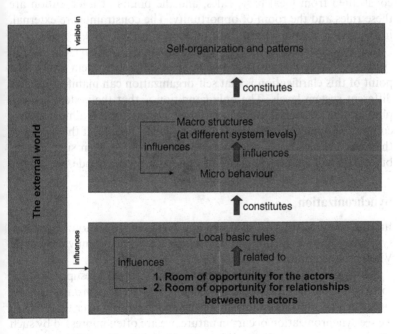

Figure 4.5 Self-organization and patterns.

The room of opportunity can be both temporary, i.e. connected to time, and connected to physical space. The room of opportunity can be affected by the geographical location of departments, location of persons on different floors of a building, etc. Although the relationship between person A and B, who works on floor 1 and floor 10 in the same building, respectively, is potentially possible, it is less likely than a relationship between A and C who work physically closer to each other. The room of opportunity for the relations between the actors is thus dependent on two factors, time and physical space. Time is linked to how often and for how long the relationship lasts, and physical space is linked to the degree of proximity regarding location.

Sub-conclusion

In this section, we have examined the following question: How can self-organization contribute to developing a culture of innovation in da Vinci organization?

A crucial insight for the management of emergent phenomena such as self-organization and culture is that 'top-down' management and hierarchical thinking will be doomed to fail. Emergent phenomena are constituted from local basic rules, and the points of intervention are these rules and the room of opportunity. The constraints are external, in the system's environment, not internal.

The macrostructures in Fig. 4.5 do not have to be at the overall system level; the macrostructure can be at different system levels. The point of this clarification is that self-organization can manifest itself at different system levels. The only condition is that the system is complex enough. A social system at different system levels is almost always complex enough for self-organization to occur, because if there is more than one (1) basic rule, and more than two people, then simple combinatorics will enable the room of opportunity to explode.[5]

Synchronization

In this section, we will examine the following question: How can synchronization contribute to developing a culture of innovation in da Vinci organization?

Self-organization and emerging phenomena often presuppose some form of synchronization of knowledge processes. Synchronization occurs when two or more things happen simultaneously over time. When we see synchronization occurs in nature, we are often impressed by such phenomena, such as a flock of birds creating a pattern in the sky, swarms of insects forming one 'unit', and so on. A similar synchronization process seems to take place in the development of knowledge when several types of knowledge are developed. We term this phenomenon 'synchronization of knowledge'. Spontaneous creative processes seem to be one of the results of synchronizing knowledge. However, there are certain conditions that need to be fulfilled for this to occur:

• Respect for each other.
• The responsibility of helping others to nurture unresolved ideas.
• Treating other people with dignity.

It is our understanding that it is three ethical factors (Baker, 1995) that are prerequisites that need to be in place for the synchronization of knowledge to be possible.

The synchronization of knowledge seems to abolish the distinctions between different types of knowledge and creates effective creative processes, which develop new knowledge, from which innovations can be developed. However, the question is how can we create a culture in a group or organization that promotes the synchronization of knowledge.

Steven Strogatz writes that "the tendency to synchronize is one of the most pervasive drives in the universe" (2004: 14). Synchronization seems to create an order, a pattern out of an apparent chaos.

What may be perceived as chaos is that we have too much information, and when it comes from many sources at once. However, in our context, it is the pattern that is of interest.

Synchronization seems to be based on three variables (Strogatz, 2004: 23):

• Threshold value
• Feedback
• Time-lag

The question we ask is: What is it that triggers and drives synchronization so that self-organization and emergent phenomena can arise and develop? If we can say something about this question, then we will have made a contribution to how self-organization and emergence arise and develop. If we consider culture and innovation as emergent phenomena, then the answer to the above question can also be used in practical contexts.

In systems other than the synchronization of knowledge, what seems to generate synchronization is a concept that Strogatz (2004: 23) terms 'absorption'. By this Strogatz means: "'absorption': a shorthand for the idea that if one oscillator kicks another over threshold, they will remain synchronized forever, as if one had absorbed the other". In social creative systems, one can imagine that respect, responsibility, and dignity (RRD) constitutes this social absorption mechanism. One can further imagine that the absorption process occurs and develops when someone genuinely exhibits RRD in relation to others. If RRD spreads throughout the system as a way of thinking, then creative energy fields will emerge, which will promote the transfer of experience. With this understanding, RRD can constitute the intervention point for initiating synchronization processes in social systems. However, RRD should also be linked to what we know about time lag, feedback, and threshold values in order for the absorption process to be as efficient as possible.

Fig. 4.6 above attempts to show that if two people (A, B) treat each other with RRD (respect, responsibility, and dignity), and one helps the other over a threshold value, which is perceived as positive by the other person, then an absorption process will have occurred between A and B, and they will be interconnected over a long period of time. If A and B exhibit RRD in relation to C, and help C over a threshold value, which is perceived as positive for C, then A, B, and C will be able to act as a 'synchronization team'. Da Vinci organizational structures can emerge in an organization, when several people in an organization exhibit RRD in relation to others facilitating absorption processes; this will create a culture for experience transfer that will promote

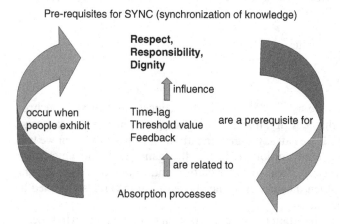

Pre-requisites for SYNC (synchronization of knowledge)

Figure 4.6 The prerequisites for the synchronization of knowledge.

innovation processes and enable the development of organizational entrepreneurship.

What can be imagined happening when RRD is established between two or more people, is a mutually reinforcing process, called 'deviation amplifying feedback' (Maruyama, 1963), where the result is qualitatively different from the sum of the parts.

In other words, it is the creative energy field that arises which is qualitatively greater than the creativity that each of the actors could create independently. This mutual reinforcement process is triggered by conscious RRD actions but develops over time into a self-organizing principle that creates emergent phenomena.

Self-organization emerges when there is explicit and clear basic rules (here RRD), which is developed through mutual reinforcement processes and absorption mechanisms resulting in emergent phenomena. This is not unlike the process that Polanyi (1983) describes about the relationship between tacit knowing processes and tacit knowledge. Polanyi's (1983) point is that there are explicit basic rules that exist in the tacit knowing processes, which can be coded, but it is not possible to make them explicit when tacit knowledge is developed.

An analogy can perhaps illustrate how this happens: If you put a new log in the fire on top of one that is burning, but half burnt through, the new log will be ignited by the old one, but the half-burnt log will also be supplied with more energy and will flare up with greater intensity.

Sub-conclusion

In this section, we have examined the following question: How can synchronization contribute to developing a culture of innovation in da Vinci organization?

When RRD is established between A and B, a mutually reinforcing process will occur, which will literally ignite A's commitment and enthusiasm. This process will unleash the creativity that no one thought existed. Together, there will be more creative energy when A and B co-create, than if A and B were to work separately, even though it initially did not look like that for B, or anyone else.

When we have more people involved in the creative energy field, than just A and B, then we will also need a greater scope of opportunity to develop all the vague ideas and unclear images, which can form the basis for the development of new knowledge processes. The creative energy fields in the organization will be able to trigger synchronization processes that will promote innovation and organizational entrepreneurship.

Main conclusion

In this chapter, we have examined the following research question: How can we utilize da Vinci's culture of innovation to promote innovation in the Fourth Industrial Revolution?

In practice, it is not the case that everyone in an organization can ignite the enthusiasm of others by showing respect, responsibility, and dignity (RRD). RRD only occurs within a few zones in an organization. In other words, there is often few creative energy fields within an organization. There are also some neutral zones, and some zones that may be called zones of the 'living dead'.

The neutral zones do not provide or consume the energy of others. They consist of individuals who work alone on their projects without involving others. The 'living dead' zones do not provide or consume the energy of others, but they also do not create anything, as do the people in the neutral zones. The 'living dead' are the people who in the literature are often called an organization's 'dead weight'. The 'black holes', on the other hand, like the black holes in the universe, absorb energy from their environment without creating or producing anything. These people may have a high degree of intensity, but like the black holes in the universe nothing emerges from them. However, they often gain the attention of the management and 'the invisible college'. They are the uncrowned 'kings of the coffee table and lunch room'. In addition, these 'black holes' put a damper on the development and spread of creative energy fields, because they are masters at tearing down unresolved images, ideas, and thoughts. The 'black holes' can also engage the interest of others, in the same way as the creative

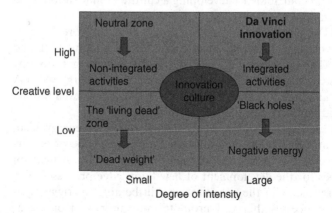

Figure 4.7 The various zones in an organization.

energy fields do, but with negative energy. The 'black holes' and the 'living dead' can team up in a cohesive critique of everything that is perceived as 'creative and new'. They often form counter-alliances to the creative energy fields, but rarely engage the neutral zones. The point, however, is that the relationships in the 'black holes' may be as strong as in the creative energy fields, but they do not develop absorption processes that lead to creativity and value creation for an organization.

Notes

1 By emergent we mean: 'Let S be a system with composition A, i.e. the various components in addition to the way they are composed. If P is a property of S, P is emergent with regard to A, if and only if no components in A possess P; otherwise P is to be regarded as a resulting property with regards to A' (Bunge, 1977: 97).
2 Balague & Elmoukliss, 2021; Brown & Eisenhardt, 2001; Stacey, 1996; Vallacher & Nowak, 1994
3 K in the figure stands for different factors at the individual, group, organizational, and societal levels, such as economic growth, economic waves, bubble formation, public opinion formation, 'there is something in the air', migration, social upheaval, cultural change, stock market crash, the importance of social groups, personally experienced happiness, personal well-being, innovations, etc. LHW stands for Long hard work. SO stands for self-organization.
4 For those who do not have 'neighbours', those at the very front and back, then only the first rule applies, and thus we will get random changes in the movement of the pattern.
5 If, for example, there are two basic rules and 10 people, then the theoretical room of opportunity will be 2 to the power of 11.

References

Adriaenssen, J-A and J-A Johannessen. "Prospect Theory as an Explanation for Resistance to Organizational Change: Some Management Implications." *Problems and Perspectives in Management*, 14, no. 2 (2016): 84–92.

Allee, V. *The Future of Knowledge*. London: Elsevier, 2003.

Baker, R. *Explaining Attitudes*. Cambridge: Cambridge University Press, 1995.

Balague, C and M Elmoukliss. *From Open to Crowd Innovation*. London: ISTE, 2021.

Bateson, G. *Steps to an Ecology of Mind*. New York: Ballantine Books, 1972.

Beer, S. *Diagnosing System for Organizing*. London: Wiley, 1985.

Brown, SL and KM Eisenhardt. *Competing on the Edge: Strategy as Structured Chaos*. Boston: Harvard Business School Press, 2001.

Bunde, M. *Fractals in Science*. London: Springer, 2013.

Bunge, M. *Treatise on Basic Philosophy. Vol. 3. Ontology I: The Furniture of the World.* Dordrecht, Holland: D. Reidel, 1977.

Bunge, M. *Philosophy of Science: From Problem to Theory.* Volume one, New Jersey: Transaction Publishers, 1998.

Cooper, J, SF Blackman, and KT Keller. *The Science of Attitudes.* London: Routledge, 2016.

Chenowelth, E. *Civil Resistance.* Oxford: OUP, 2020.

Gelb, M. *How to Think Like Leonardo Da Vinci: Seven Steps to Genius Everyday.* New York: Element Books, 2004.

Klein, G. *The Power of Intuition.* New York: Currency Doubleday, 2003.

Liker, JK. *The Toyota Way.* New York: McGraw-Hill, 2004.

Maruyama, M. "The Second Cybernetics, Deviating-amplifying Mutual Causal Processes." *American Scientist*, 51 (1963): 164–179.

Miller, JG *Living Systems.* New York: McGraw-Hill, 1978.

Polanyi, M. *The Tacit Dimension.* New York: Smith, 1983.

Stacey, RD. *Complexity and Creativity in Organizations.* San Francisco: Berrett-Koehler, 1996.

Schweitzer, F (Ed.). *Self-Organization of Complex Structures: from Individual to Collective Dynamics, Part 2: Biological and Ecological Dynamic, Socio Economic Processes.* London: Gordon and Breach, 1997.

Schweitzer, F and J Zimmermann. "Communication and Self-organization in Complex Systems: A Basic Approach" In *Knowledge, Complexity and Innovation Systems*, edited by MM Fisher & J Frøhlich, 275–296. Heidelberg: Springer, 2001.

Strogatz, S. *Sync: The Emerging Science of Spontaneous Order.* New York: Penguin Books, 2004.

Vallacher, R and A Nowak (Ed.). *Dynamical Systems in Social Psychology.* New York: Academic Press, 1994.

5 Da Vinci motivation as enthusiasm

Key points in this chapter

- The success of organizations in the future will to a large degree be determined by their ability to bring creative people on board.
- Employees who feel they are being 'seen and heard' will tend to be more engaged and perform better; consequently, recognition, respect, and dignity, will be important tools in the leader's toolbox.
- Enthusiasm and commitment are crucial factors that positively affect creativity, performance, and the achievement of an organization's purpose.
- The enthusiastic and mindful person is 'present in the moment'. This person is also optimistic and has a positive image of the future.
- 90% of the factors that are crucial to success stem from the attitude one has to challenges and problems.
- Be authentic and say yes to fewer things.
- If you are going to put together a really creative group, then you should search for people who have a basic optimistic attitude, and believe they can solve problems.

Introduction

According to Wright (2006), one of the criteria for a company's success is the level of its employees' job satisfaction. Job satisfaction is, however, a complex construct, which does not have a single unambiguous definition. Contentment, fulfilment, and well-being are all words that have been used in the attempt to encompass something of what one is trying to get to grips with when using the term 'job satisfaction' (Seligman, 2011: 5–26). Job satisfaction has been a focus

DOI: 10.4324/9781003335726-5

area in positive psychology (Seligman, 2002) and positive leadership (Cameron et al., 2003) for a relatively long time.

Significant changes are happening to the design and context of jobs in the global knowledge economy (Grant & Parker, 2009). The type of behaviour demanded of employees is also changing. In addition to high levels of expertise, companies are seeking positive employees who are committed and optimistic (Kesebir & Diener, 2008; Peterson et al., 2005).

Many of the classic research studies have been oriented around the question of what job characteristics motivate employees (Grant & Parker, 2009: 318; Grant & Ashford, 2008). Positive psychology is concerned with the personal characteristics that will promote job satisfaction and accordingly motivate employees. Proactive behaviour (Grant & Spence, 2010) and pro-social behaviour appear to promote job satisfaction. Reasons advanced to explain this fact include the idea that these types of behaviour transmit to other employees, creating enthusiasm and commitment, which generates positive reinforcement (Grant, 2007).

How employees are treated is decisive for whether a workplace becomes a place that induces sickness among employees, or a place where people develop job satisfaction and well-being, which they take with them beyond the workplace (Robertson & Cooper, 2011:3). Job satisfaction is linked to many factors, both within and outside the workplace (Danna & Griffin, 1999). These factors may be classified into four categories:

1　**Social factors**: meaningful relationships, the ability to manage stress, commitment, curiosity, amiability, a sense of well-being, etc. (Bruke & Cooper, 2008; Dewe & Cooper, 2012: 4; Boxall & Purcell, 2010; Robertson & Cooper, 2011: 4–10)
2　**Political factors**: involvement, participation, co-determination, employee consultation, etc. (Beach & Connolly, 2005; Gardner et al., 2011; Wegge et al., 2010)
3　**Material factors**: financial factors, physical health, access to technology, competence, etc. (Adler et al., 1999; Brynjolfsson & McAfee, 2014; Innerarity, 2012; Robertson & Cooper, 2011: 11).
4　**Cultural factors**: Meaningful work, organizational norms, and values that accord with the employee's own norms and values (Alveson, 2000; Godard, 2010; Kehoe & Wright, 2013; Luthans et al., 2015).

In this chapter, we will focus solely on the social factors. Within this category, we opt to examine in greater depth the impact of an enthusiastic employee on job satisfaction and well-being in the workplace (Mintzberg, 2019).

Envisage a future workplace where all the employees are inquisitive, very committed, help each other, are good-humoured, and experience satisfaction in their everyday work. Cameron et al. (2003:3) contrast such an organization with a workplace that is characterized by greed, egoism, and manipulation and where the main focus is on the financial bottom line. Which of these organizations would you want to work for?

Working life in the future will be characterized by the battle for talented people. In all probability, such people will choose to work for businesses with high levels of job satisfaction (Compton & Hoffman, 2012; Danna & Griffin, 1999).

A large-scale empirical study on job satisfaction showed that people who were uncertain as to whether their job was secure showed lower levels of satisfaction, commitment, and responsibility in their current job (Sora et al., 2009). Among other things, this means that the trend that we are seeing in the global labour market towards reduced job security is affecting workers' commitment and accordingly is indirectly affecting companies' performance (Standing, 2014).

The characteristic feature of organizations in the global knowledge economy is the fact that they are undergoing constant processes of change (Kehoe & Wright, 2013). These processes are often experienced as threatening and negative (Harter et al., 2003). In this context, it may be important to focus on the positive aspects of continual change processes (Liker & Ross, 2016). This is one of the areas where positive psychology may have a contribution to make (Dewe & Cooper, 2012: 6). Employees who feel that they are noticed, who work largely autonomously, and who have the opportunity to experience well-being and satisfaction in the workplace, will be more engaged and perform better (Mintzberg, 2019; Oswald & Wu, 2010).

The problem we will investigate in this chapter is as follows: How can enthusiasm be utilized as da Vinci motivation to promote innovation in the Fourth Industrial Revolution?

The introduction is visualized in Fig. 5.1, which is intended to highlight the association between enthusiasm and organizational goal achievement, to underline that enthusiasm and job satisfaction have clear organizational functions. First, we will discuss the concept of 'enthusiasm'. Thereafter, we will analyze and discuss 'enthusiasm'.

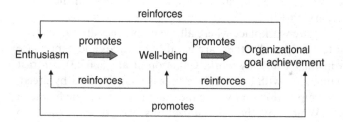

Figure 5.1 Enthusiasm, job satisfaction, and organizational goal achievement.

Enthusiasm

Explanation

Commitment and enthusiasm are closely related concepts (West, 2012). For pedagogical reasons, we make no distinction between these two concepts but use them interchangeably.

One often hears statements of the type: 'You can't be more enthusiastic than you feel'. Of course, this is true, but you can become more enthusiastic than you are now, if you wish. Managers should be aware of this because enthusiasm promotes goal achievement and increases the cohesion of the group (Lynn & Snyder, 2005). Peale (1994: 427) expresses this in the following way: "The important fact is that you can deliberately make yourself enthusiastic". This is Peale's '*As if*' principle (Peale, 1994: 428), which can be used to increase enthusiasm. This is also underlined by Kehoe & Wright (2013: 381), who also stress that acting as if you are enthusiastic, leads to you becoming more enthusiastic.

Harter et al. (2003: 205–224) have conducted a major empirical study where they looked at the relationship between commitment, enthusiasm, and job satisfaction. They found that where the relationship was very good, there was also a higher probability of customer and client loyalty, higher productivity, lower turnover rates, and higher organizational goal achievement. This indicates that enthusiasm and commitment are crucial factors that influence job satisfaction and organizational goal achievement (Mintzberg, 2019). This has also been substantiated by Vogelaar (2010, 2016, 2016a).

One of the secrets to becoming more enthusiastic is to do more of what others don't do, i.e. develop your uniqueness. This may be promoted by thinking differently than others in relation to strategy (Kim & Mauborgne, 2005). You can also connect themes and problem areas that have not previously been connected (Peale, 1994: 272), and consequently, create that which is innovative and new.

To promote enthusiasm, you should say yes to fewer things. The reason for this action plan is that enthusiasm almost invariably leads to new opportunities emerging. The explanation here is that the enthusiastic person attracts others who want to work with him/her. In such a situation, if he/her does not learn to say yes to fewer things, there is a risk of being enthusiastic one moment, and burned out the next (Vogelaar, 2016). To say yes to fewer things, we call here flexibility. The aim is therefore to seek a balance that enhances enthusiasm without becoming overworked (Vallerand, 2015).

Enthusiasm is also promoted when a person is authentic, someone who is the 'real deal'. The authentic individual stands by his values regardless of the situation; and he/she creates enthusiasm in others by his/her manner (Boyle, 2004), and example (Harter et al., 2003: 389). The authentic individual creates an aura of safety around himself/herself, by not pretending to be something he/she isn't by putting up a false facade (York, 2014).

The enthusiastic person often focuses his/her awareness on the present moment, i.e. he/she exhibits mindfulness (Karremans & Papies, 2017). One focuses especially on the present moment when one is in 'the flow zone' (Csikszentmihalyi, 2002).

The enthusiastic person not only focuses his/her awareness on the present moment but he/she is also optimistic and has a positive image of the future (Seligman, 2006). An important point concerning optimism (Seligman, 2006) is that we can teach ourselves to be more optimistic, and managers can develop action plans to facilitate this. From a management perspective, this is important because the optimistic person engenders enthusiasm in others, which leads to better job satisfaction (Weich, 2016), which is directly related to increased organizational performance (Wright, 2006).

In Fig. 5.2, we have shown our explanation of enthusiasm. The model also shows how we have organized the analysis and discussion of enthusiasm in the following.

Analysis and discussion

We will examine the five elements in Fig. 5.2 in the analysis and discussion.

Uniqueness (doing what others don't do)

When you notice that you continually have to do more to achieve desired results, then you should stop and change your perspective and

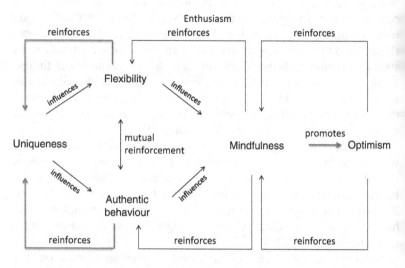

Figure 5.2 Enthusiasm.

working methods, because this is the moment you have the opportunity to do things differently (Scott & Hoffman, 2015). Doing what others don't do is a skill that can be developed and learned. On the organizational level, Kim and Mauborgne (2005) explain the strategy. At the individual level, one can use Leonardo da Vinci's seven principles (Gelb, 2004). These principles are to: develop an insatiable curiosity; learn from experience; focus on the present moment; embrace uncertainty; continually alternate between part and whole; keep yourself physically fit and search for patterns in everything.

To build uniqueness at both individual and organizational levels, you can deliberately put yourself in situations that increase the pressure to do things in a unique way (Habegger, 2016). Such situations make it possible to withdraw and reflect on your own reactions, as well as trying to do things different from the usual working methods. When increasing the pressure on yourself by becoming involved in such practical experiments, you will develop the expertise that will enable you to do things differently from others, which will promote success (Gelb, 2004; Kim & Mauborgne, 2005). In this way, you will manage to cope with pressure in a more adequate way (Habegger, 2016). By continually taking yourself out of your comfort zone, and experimenting by reacting differently than you would normally do in such situations, you will be able to move to a higher level of competence regarding solution strategies (Dryden, 2012).

It is attitudes towards the challenges and problems that often separate those who succeed from those who don't succeed (Abattzidis, 2015; Danna & Griffin, 1999). Some researchers claim that more than 90% of the factors that are critical to success come from the attitude you have to challenges, problems, and phenomena (Peale, 1994: 312). The attitudes that stand out positively says Peale (1994: 312) are:

* To try, try, try
* To never give up
* To persevere

This is also what the psychologist Dweck (2012) found were important factors for being successful. Her research shows specifically that there are four factors that are essential for success: to have a clear burning desire, to persevere, to have moral courage, and self-discipline.

Doing what others don't do, strengthens identity, attracts attention from the outside world, and fosters the presentation of oneself (Codol, 1984). Snyder and Fromkin (1980) have developed a theory explaining that people strive to be unique, because they feel uncomfortable being too similar to others. Enthusiasm is also reinforced when one experiences that one is unique (Snyder & Lopez, 2007).

One may be unique in many areas, such as in relation to attitudes, creativity, personality, judgement, experience, belonging, consumption, etc. Some research highlights that belonging to smaller groups satisfies the need for uniqueness better than belonging to larger groups (Lynn & Snyder, 2005: 396).

People tend to seek to be unique within areas that are socially acceptable, and to a lesser extent in those areas that are not socially acceptable (Ditto & Griffin, 1993). The explanation is that one is socially rewarded when one excels in areas that are socially accepted, which reinforces enthusiasm.

What we have described here with reference to empirical research may be expressed in the sentence: Enthusiasm increases when you do what others don't do. Thus, based on this understanding, enthusiasm is not something you have or don't have, it is a resource that may be strengthened by striving to be unique. Enthusiasm may be understood as a social mechanism that 'makes everything different' (Peale, 1994: 411), or as 'the difference which makes a difference' (Bateson, 1972: 272).

Flexibility (saying yes to fewer things)

When you say yes to fewer things you increase your flexibility, because you can focus more on what you are really interested in, your burning desire (Dweck, 2012). This flexibility promotes creativity and increases enthusiasm, and results in a greater ability to solve problems (Isen, 1999).

When you have more flexibility, you have greater control over your own situation (Media, 2016). This in turn promotes personal mastery (Isen, 2005). If you feel that you are being controlled, this will reduce your level of performance (Bandura, 1997).

In order to say yes to fewer things, you have to withdraw from people that increase your stress level and fill you with negative energy (Isen, 2005).

Just as you should have a list of the critical activities that you have to do the following day, you should also have a list of those activities you should avoid, so you don't drain yourself of energy (Dweck, 2012). To draft such lists, the following questions may be of help. The list is analogous to Dweck's (2012) ideas concerning personal growth:

- What am I trying to achieve?
- Why I believe that what I am trying to achieve, can be achieved?
- What makes me believe that it's not possible to achieve a specific goal?
- What can I lose and what do I gain by trying?
- Can I spend more time and more energy if I focused on other goals?

When you encounter opposition a good strategy is to give enough rope to those people who impede your way to goal, so that they reveal their intentions and plans (Media, 2016). Ask them for help, and you'll most likely change their behaviour towards you. Ask them for more help, and you'll have turned an opponent into a teammate (Syed, 2016).

The key to enthusiasm is that you do what you really want to do (Dweck, 2012). You affect others with your behaviour, whether it is enthusiastic, critical, or negative (Lewis, 2000). Just as the enthusiastic teacher inspires his students, the manager inspires his staff with his enthusiasm or lack of it. On the other hand, you are also affected by the enthusiasm of others or lack of it. However, you have control over how you react towards the behaviour of others. It is how you react to others' enthusiasm or lack of enthusiasm, which can change the development of a relationship and situation (Syed, 2016).

Authentic (being yourself)

Being authentic means being yourself, and not using 'brands, fakes, and spin' (Boyle, 2004: 15). The authentic person doesn't hide behind a facade, but is himself/herself without pretending to be something he/she isn't (York, 2014). This makes it easier for others to be open towards him/her (Joseph, 2016). The authentic person isn't manipulative or calculating in his/her behaviour (Thacker, 2016), and he/she expresses his/her own thoughts and feelings that stimulates enthusiasm and infects others (Harter et al., 2003: 389).

One may be prevented from being authentic because of the wish to act rationally (Knapp & Hulbert, 2016). Rational behaviour to a degree negates feelings, while the authentic and enthusiastic person connects to their feelings (Joseph, 2016; York, 2014).

Today, the trend is that you present yourself in such a way that you gain acceptance by others (Boyle, 2004). However, this can easily undermine being authentic and enthusiastic (York, 2014). Thus, we present ourselves so others will believe we are competent (Joseph, 2016), and we try to gain respect by presenting ourselves the way others wish us to be and not necessarily how we are (Knapp & Hulbert, 2016).

Today, it is perhaps the trend that one presents oneself in such a way that one seeks acceptance by others (Boyle, 2004). This behaviour can easily thwart being authentic and enthusiastic (York, 2014). We present ourselves in such a way so others will believe that we are competent (Joseph, 2016). We try therefore to win others' respect by presenting ourselves as we wish to be perceived, and the way others want us to be, not necessarily the way we actually are (Knapp & Hulbert, 2016).

Being authentic is not easy today when expectations are very demanding regarding the various roles one has to play (Thacker, 2016). However, being authentic does not mean that our behaviour will be the same in different roles and in different contexts. It simply means that one should distinguish between the roles in real life and the roles played in 'life's theatre' (Boyle, 2004).

The term 'role' is a metaphor derived from the theatre. Of course, your various roles in real life does not imply the theatrical use of the word. Such confusion would lead to high psychological stress levels, and ultimately to collapse (Joseph, 2016; Syed, 2016). You should be yourself in the various roles you take on (Thacker, 2016). It is when you confuse roles in reality with roles in the dramatic sense of the word that authenticity is threatened (Joseph, 2016; Knapp & Hulbert, 2016).

Even when you are faced with different expectations in your various roles, this does not mean that you should act like a social chameleon. You may adapt to your different roles, but you should not change your basic values from role to role (Joseph, 2016). Your basic values act as your anchor and standing by them makes you appear authentic in your various roles (Knapp & Hulbert, 2016).

Mindfulness (present-moment awareness)

Being mindful may be understood and experienced in many ways. At the micro level, it may be the small moments of intensity and proximity to the matter at hand. Mindfulness can also be experienced in a conversation (Karremans & Papies, 2017); and it is often in dialogues we have present-moment awareness (Greenberg, 2016).

Csikszentmihalyi (2002) uses the expression being 'in flow' when one is completely absorbed in what one is doing, so that time and place disappear. In this 'flow zone', both boredom and anxiety disappear, and one becomes one with the matter at hand.

In the flow zone, challenges and problems are turned into opportunities where immediate feedback on performance is critical to remaining in the zone (Csikszentmihalyi, 1996, 1997). Continuous feedback on your performance is crucial, because you are focused on the present, and can adjust your behaviour immediately (Bell, 2017). This enhances concentration and sensibility in relation to the task you are performing (Greenberg, 2016). In the flow zone, you have a heightened sense of present-moment awareness. You let yourself go and your energy is transmitted to the present challenge (Karremans & Papies, 2017). Being in the flow zone is characterized by the feeling that you have control over how the situation will develop (Csikszentmihalyi, 1997), and time is perceived as going faster than normal (Nakamura & Csikszentmihalyi, 2005: 90).

It is not the goal in itself that is important when you are mindful, but the inner rewards of mastering a situation (Karremans & Papies, 2017). In such a condition, you perform at the very limit of your capacity. To be in a state of mindfulness it is important that your skills harmonise with the challenges. Nakamura and Csikszentmihalyi (2005: 90) comment: "If the challenges exceed skills, one first becomes vigilant, and then anxious". However, if the opposite is the case, "if skills exceed challenges one first relaxes and eventually becomes bored" (Ibid). Thus, to be mindful over time you must either lower your level of ambition or increase the challenges. Transferred to the area of management this involves giving immediate feedback, and being aware of balancing a person's resources with the tasks to be performed.

Having present-moment awareness is similar to being in the flow zone. We are intensely focused on what we are doing. To remain in this condition it is necessary to limit incoming signals to what we are focused on. All other signals will be perceived as noise, and can easily distract us and lead us out of the flow zone (Karremans & Papies, 2017).

Being in the flow zone, which is an aspect of being mindful, is perceived as a reward in itself, 'and leads the individual to seek to replicate
flow experiences' (Nakamura & Csikszentmihalyi, 2005: 92). To move
into the flow zone, it is essential that one's skills and interests match and
are connected to a specific interest (Csikszentmihalyi, 1997).

Research indicates (Nakamura & Csikszentmihalyi, 2005: 92) that
students who experience being in the flow zone early in a course will
perform better at the end of the course. The longer students are in the
zone, the more this enhances their self-esteem and performance (Wells,
1988). In general, when planning projects, managers should ensure
that employees have the opportunity of entering the zone at an early
point.

Optimism

Optimists are people who expect that good things will happen to them
(Carver & Scheier, 2005). Optimism is thus related to future expectations (Seligman, 2006). In a research context, this may be related to
expectancy-value models of motivation (Heinrichs et al., 2013). These
models start with the assumption that behaviour is organized around
the pursuit of goals, and the goals are related to values. The more
important a goal is, the greater the value for the individual's motivation (Arnold & Klein, 2017). The second element of these models is
expectations: the confidence or doubts related to whether the goals are
attainable. Only those with a sufficient degree of confidence concerning the possibility of achieving the goals will take measures to
accomplish them (Heinrichs et al., 2013: 45–47). The optimist has this
confidence, the pessimist does not (Seligman, 2006).

Can you learn to be more optimistic? Yes, says Seligman (2006).
One of the reasons why you should seek to be more optimistic is that
the optimistic person is more motivated to achieve goals than the
pessimist (Chase, 2016: 56), and, in addition, also has a greater experience of a more meaningful life, says Seligman (2006: iv).

It is largely how we relate to the challenges and situations we meet,
which determines how we deal with them, not necessarily the challenges and situations in themselves (Arnold & Klein, 2017: 13–15).
While pessimism is closely related to a negative self-image, optimism is
closely related to a positive self-image (Seligman, 2006: 33–45).

There are some things we can control, and other things we can't
control. For instance, we have no control over how others will react in
relation to us. On the other hand, we have complete control over how
we react towards the behaviour of others.

We can do something about the way we think, speak and act, and thereby also affect or influence others. If we, for example, think that we have no possibility of changing others, then the chances are that this will become a self-fulfilling prophecy (Weich, 2016). However, if we think we can change people's behaviour by changing our own reactions to their behaviour, we will be able to change others (Seligman, 2016).

Our habitual way of thinking, speaking and acting is not something that is a pattern that is carved in stone. It is more like a pattern frozen into ice, and ice melts in *the sun*. The sun in this case being the smile and commitment that infects others (Chase, 2016).

Seligman (2006: 8) states that one of the clearest findings in psychology over the past thirty years is that individuals can choose the way they think and the way they react to others' behaviour. If we relate this to recent brain research (Kreiman et al., 2000), it becomes apparent that how we think affects our behaviour, and we can freely choose to think differently (Greenberg, 2016). It is all a matter of wanting to be optimistic and framing the outside world from this perspective.

Heredity and environment impact on how we think. However, Seligman (2006), Kreiman et al. (2000) and Greenberg (2016) make the point that we can choose how we relate to our own thinking, which affects our behaviour. This insight reduces the importance of both heredity and the environment. In the situation one finds oneself in at any given time, heredity and environment will be given quantities. On the other hand, we have a degree of freedom regarding how we choose to think. It is this degree of freedom that determines whether we frame the outside world from an optimistic or pessimistic perspective. By choosing an optimistic perspective, we change established patterns of behaviour, although this may take time.

The common belief is that achievement is a result of talent, desires, interests, and goal orientation. However, Seligman (2006: 13) says that failure may also occur when talent and a burning desire are present in abundance but optimism is lacking. Talent and a burning desire to perform at a high level are obviously important, but without an optimistic attitude then it can all be for nothing.

If you think that nothing helps no matter what you do then you have developed a basic pessimistic attitude, or what is called 'learned helplessness' (Seligman, 1975). In other words, whenever you are faced with any difficulties you easily give up. You don't look for opportunities but only for limitations (Seligman, 2006: 23). Learned helplessness also leads to passivity (Seligman, 1975), and individuals tend to explain difficulties they meet as something they don't master.

When individuals experience lack of control, they look for causes. They often find causes that may differ considerably from the real causes why things went wrong (Linley & Joseph, 2004). This mistaken causality is thus 'frozen solid', and is used by the individual to explain why things were unsuccessful. However, the truth is that one selects one or more causes that do not necessarily correspond to reality. When these faulty causes are established, they are perceived as 'the truth' by the individual in question. If, however, one learns that optimism can be an important factor, then you can become immunized against faulty reasoning, passivity, and learned helplessness (Weich, 2016).

Seligman (2006: 44–54) has identified six elements that explain whether we have a basic pessimistic or optimistic attitude. A pessimistic attitude seeks permanent, universal, and external explanations, while an optimistic attitude seeks temporary, specific, and internal explanations.

It is how we think in relation to these elements that says something about whether we have a pessimistic or an optimistic attitude. The good news, which cannot be said often enough, is that a basic pessimistic attitude can be changed, and changed so that it lasts. It is how we choose to think, that determines how we feel, and this affects the development of our basic attitude (Weich, 2016). A technique to change our basic attitude from pessimistic to optimistic is to perform an optimistic personal dialogue (Seligman, 2006). Another technique is to focus on a burning desire, develop perseverance in relation to this desire, work with moral courage in relation to the burning desire, and develop self-discipline (Dweck, 2012; Weich, 2016).

In practice, there is a clear relationship between people who think they can solve problems and challenges, and those who think they can't. In any work situation, you should try to be part of the solution and not part of the problem. The optimistic person is more likely to be viewed as part of the solution, while the pessimistic person is seen as being part of the problem (Arnold & Klein, 2017).

If you have to put together a really creative group, you should search for those people who have a basic optimistic attitude and think they can solve the problem (Dweck, 2012). The explanation is that optimistic people are more likely to succeed because they don't give up, but keep going until the problem is solved, in spite of difficulties (Weich, 2016).

How can a pessimist become an optimist?

Seligman (2006: 207) says that if you suffer a personal defeat you should carry out an inner dialogue with yourself and play it in your inner theatre from a more encouraging position, even if you do not feel like doing it at that moment in time. You need to look at setbacks as temporary and specific, not as permanent and universal. A universal attitude may be exemplified by statements of the type: Everyone thinks that; everybody does it; it is something everyone knows; etc. Permanent attitudes can be described with statements of the type: that's just the way it is; it has always been like that; etc.

However, there are some situations where a basic pessimistic attitude can be used to advantage. Such situations include when one plans and acts in risky, uncertain, and ambiguous situations. The same applies if one wants to seem polite in situations where others are in great difficulty. In such situations, one should try to understand the other's perspective and the situation the other is in, and not adopt an optimistic attitude (Seligman, 2006: 207). To start with an optimistic attitude in such situations would be counterproductive. On the other hand, at a later point, one can use simple optimistic techniques to show the other that there is light at the end of the tunnel.

When we meet opposition, we often react by letting our thoughts revolve around the problems we encounter. Our thoughts freeze relatively quickly to a particular perception of the situation, which in many cases may be characterized as an automatic process triggered by habitual thinking linked to similar situations we have encountered. This has consequences for both our emotions and our actions (Seligman, 2006: 211; Dweck, 2012).

To escape from this negative spiral, the first step is to reflect on the link between the opposition we face, and the judgements we automatically choose to make, and the feelings and actions this leads to, as well as the consequences this has for us. Thus, every time we meet opposition, we should separate the problems we encounter from our 'automatic' thoughts and behaviour patterns (Weich, 2016). Doing what others don't expect us to do is an aid in achieving this, because others expect us to do what they have experienced we've done before. The point of this method is to make a counterfactual intervention, to change other people's expectations (Watzlawick et al., 2011).

To find out how the opposition we meet triggers thoughts, perceptions, emotions, actions, and consequences, a simple strategy may be of help. This involves writing a diary in which over time you will be able to see a pattern of how you think and act in different situations. After two or three weeks, a pattern will be revealed. You will then be able to attempt to disengage your automatic responses in such situations. This is a technique strongly recommended by

Seligman (2006: 213). The point is to change your automatic response into a deliberate and thoughtful action.

The pessimistic explanatory habit will often in its social consequences seem passive and the person will often withdraw from the situation. The optimistic explanation method will, as a rule, energize the situation (Seligman, 2006: 216; Arnold & Klein, 2017).

Basically, there are two main ways of promoting a transition from a pessimistic to a basic optimistic attitude, says Seligman (2006: 217):

1 Distraction. When a sequence of pessimistic thinking and actions starts, distract it automatically by deliberately framing the situation differently.

2 Arguments. Carry out an 'inner-argument' against your own thoughts in relation to the situation.

   a Check the facts
   b Identify options
   c Examine the consequences
   d Find out how useful any action may be

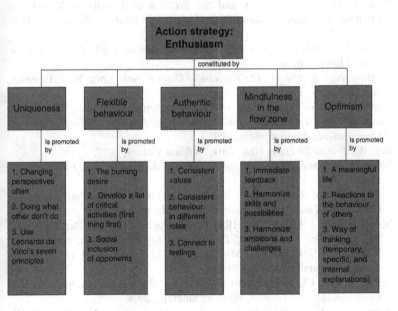

Figure. 5.3 An analytical framework representing an action plan for creating enthusiasm.

Conclusion

The problem for discussion in this chapter was the following: How can enthusiasm be utilized as da Vinci motivation to promote innovation in the Fourth Industrial Revolution?

The enthusiastic person will tend to infect others with their enthusiasm, thus intensifying enthusiasm in work situations.

There are five areas we have focused on that encourage enthusiasm: uniqueness, flexibility, authentic behaviour, mindfulness in the flow zone as well as optimism.

We have explained three subgroups within each of the five areas. We have systematized the three subgroups within each of the five areas in Fig. 5.3. Fig. 5.3 may also be understood as an overall action strategy that responds to the problem we have discussed in this chapter.

References

Abattzidis, M. *Life Outside Your Comfort Zone.* New York: Create Space, 2015.

Adler, P, B Goldoftas and D Levine. "Flexibility versus Efficiency? A Case Study of Model Changeovers in the Toyota Production System." *Organizational Science*, 10 (1999): 43–68.

Alveson, M. "Social Identity and the Problem of Loyalty in Knowledge Intensive Companies." *Journal of Management Studies*, 37, no. 8 (2000): 1101–1123.

Arnold, J and B Klein. *Think Big: Overcoming Obstacles with Optimism.* New York: Howard Books, 2017.

Bandura, A. *Self-efficacy: The Exercise of Control.* New York: W.H. Freeman and Company, 1997.

Bateson, G. *Steps to an Ecology of Mind.* London: Intex Books, 1972.

Beach, LR and T Connolly. *The Psychology of Decision Making: People in Organizations.* London: Sage, 2005.

Bell, R. *How to Be Here.* New York: William Collins, 2017.

Boyle, D. *Authenticity: Brands, Fakes, Spin and the Lust for Real Life.* London: Harper, 2004.

Bowles, D and CL Cooper. *Employee Morale: Driving Performance in Challenging Times.* Basingstoke: Palgrave Macmillan, 2009.

Boxall, PF and J Purcell. "An HRM Perspective on Employee Participation." In *The Oxford Handbook of Participation in Organizations*, edited by A Wilkinson, PJ Golan, M Marchington& D Lewins, 129–151. Oxford: Oxford University Press. s. 2010.

Bruke, R and CL Cooper (eds.). *The Long Work hours Culture: Causes, Consequences, and Choices.* Bingley: Emerald, 2008.

Brynjolfsson, E and A McAfee. *The Second Machine Age.* New York: W.W. Norton, 2014.

Cameron, KS, JE Dutton, and RE Quinn. "Foundations of Positive Organizational Scholarship." In *Positive Organizational Scholarship*, edited by KS Cameron, JE Dutton & RE Quinn, 3–13. London: Berret Koehler, BK, 2003.

Carver, CS and MF Scheier. "Optimism." In *Handbook of Positive Psychology*, edited by CR Snyder and SJ Lopez, 231–243. New York: Oxford University Press, 2005.

Chase, A. *Positive Thinking*. New York: CreateSpace, 2016.

Codol, J-P. "Social Differentiation and Non-differentiation." In *The Social Dimension*, edited by H Taifel. Cambridge: Cambridge University Press, 1984.

Compton, C and E Hoffman. *Positive Psychology: The Science of Happiness and Flourishing*. London: Wordsworth Publishing, 2012.

Csikszentmihalyi, M. *Creativity*. New York: Harper Collins, 1996.

Csikszentmihalyi, M. *Finding Flow*. New York: Basic Books, 1997.

Csikszentmihalyi, M. *Flow*. London: Rider, 2002.

Danna, K and RW Griffin. "Health and Well-Being in the Workplace: A Review and Synthesis of the Literature." *Journal of Management*, 25, no. 3 (1999): 357–384.

Ditto, PH and J Griffin. "The Value of Uniqueness." *Journal of Social Behavior and Personality*, 8 (1993): 221–240.

Dryden, W. *How to Come Out of Your Comfort Zone*. London: Sheldon Press, 2012.

Dewe, P and C Cooper. *Well-Being and Work*. London: Palgrave Macmillan, 2012.

Dweck, CS. *Mindset*. New York: Robinson, 2012.

Førsterling, F. *Attribution, an Introduction to Theories, Research and Applications*. London: Routledge, 2001.

Gardner, TM, PM Wright, and LM Moynihan. "The Impact of Motivation, Empowerment, and Skill Enhancing Practices on Aggregate Voluntary Turnover: The Mediating Effect of Collective Affective Commitment." *Personnel Psychology*, 64 (2011):315–350.

Gelb, MJ. *How to Think Like Leonardo da Vinci*. New York: Delacorte Press, 2004.

Godard, J. "What Is Best for workers? the Implication of Workplace and Human Resource Management Practices Revisited." *Industrial Relations*, 49, no. 3 (2010):466–488.

Graham, S and VS Folkes (eds.). *Attribution Theory*. New York: Psychology Press, 2016.

Grant, AM. "Relational Job Design and the Motivation to Make a Prosocial Difference." *Academy of Management Review*, 32 (2007):393–417.

Grant, AM and SJ Ashford. "The Dynamics of Proactivity at Work." *Research in Organizational Behavior*, 28 (2008): 3–34.

Grant, AM and SK Parker. "Redesigning Work Design theories: The Rise of relational and Proactive Perspectives." *The Academy of Management Annals*, 3 (2009): 317–375.

Grant, AM and GB Spence. "Using coaching and Positive Psychology to Promote a Flourishing Workforce: A Model of Goal-striving and Mental Health."In *Oxford Handbook of Positive Psychology and Work*, edited by PA Linley, S Harrington & N Garcea, 175–188. Oxford: Oxford University Press, 2010.

Grant, RM. "The Knowledge-Based View of the Firm." In *The Oxford Handbook of Strategy*, edited by D Faulkner & A Campbell, 203–231. Oxford: Oxford University Press, 2003.

Greenberg, M. *The Stress-proof Brain: Master Your Emotional Response to Stress Using Mindfulness and Neuroplasticity*. New York: New Harbinger, 2016.

Griffin MA and SK Parker. "A New Model of Work Role Performance: Positive Behavior in Uncertain and Interdependent Contexts." *Academy of Management Journal*, 50 (2007): 327–347.

Habegger, L. *Authority Positioning: How to Become the Leader in Your Niche*. New York: Your Epic Book, 2016.

Harter, JK, FL Schmidt, and CLM Keyes. "Well-Being in the Workplace and Its Relationship to Business Outcomes: A Review of the Gallup Studies." In *Flourishing: The Positive Person and the Good Life*, edited by CLM Keyes & J Haid, 205–224. Washington DC: American Psychological Association, 2003.

Heinrichs, K, F Oser, and T Lovat. *Handbook of Moral Motivation: Theories, Models, Application*. New York: Sense Publisher, 2013.

Hiroto, DS. "Locus of Control and Learned Helplessness." *Journal of Experimental Psychology*, 102 (1974): 187–193.

Innerarity, D. "Power and Knowledge: The Politics of the Knowledge Society." *European Journal of Social Theory*, 16, no. 1 (2012): 3–16.

Isen, AM. "On the Relationship between Affect and Creative problem solving." In *Affect, Creative Experience, and Psychological Adjustment*, edited by S Russ, 3–17. Philadelphia: Taylor and Francis, 1999.

Isen. AM. "A Role of Neurophysiology in Understanding the facilitating Influence of Positive Affect on Social Behavior and Cognitive Processes." In *Handbook of Positive Psychology*, edited by CR Snyder and SJ Lopez, 528–540. New York. N.Y. US: Oxford University Press, 2005.

James, W. *Talks to Teachers on Psychology*. Cambridge, MA: Harvard University Press, 1983.

Joseph, S. *Authentic: How to Be Yourself and Why It Matters*. New York: Platkus, 2016.

Karremans, J and E Papies (eds.). *Mindfulness in Social Psychology*. London: Routledge, 2017.

Kashdan, TB and PJ Silvia. "Curiosity and Interest: The Benefits of thriving on Novelty and Challenge." In *The Oxford Handbook of Positive Psychology*, edited by SJ Lopez & CR Snyder, 367–374. Oxford: Oxford University Press, 2011.

Kehoe, RR and PM Wright. "The Impact of High Performance Human Resource Practices on Employees Attitudes and behaviors." *Journal of Management*, 39, no. 2 (2013): 366–391.

Kesebir, P and E Diener. "In Pursuit of Happiness: Empirical Answers to Philosophical Questions." *Perspectives on Psychological Science*, 3 (2008):117–125.

Kim, WC and R Mauborgne. *Blue Ocean Strategy*. Boston: Harvard Business School Press, 2005.

Kirzner, IM. *Competition and Entrepreneurship*. Chicago: The University of Chicago Press, 1973.

Kirzner, IM. *Perception, Opportunity, and Profit: Studies in the Theory and Entrepreneurship*. Chicago: University of Chicago Press, 1979.

Kirzner, IM. "The Theory of Entrepreneurship in Economic Growth." In *Encyclopedia of Entrepreneurship*, edited by CA Kent, DL Sexton, and KH Vesper. N.J: Prentice Hall, Englewood Cliffs, 1982.

Knapp, JC and A Hulbert. *Ghost-Writing and the Ethics of Authenticity*. London: Palgrave, 2016.

Kreiman, G, C Koch and I Fried. "Imagery Neurons in the Human Brain." *Nature*, 408 (2000): 357–361.

Lewis, T. *A General Theory of Love*. New York: Random House, 2000.

Liker, J. *The Toyota Way*. New York: McGraw-Hill, 2004.

Liker, J and K Ross. *The Toyota Way to Service Excellence, Lean Transformation in Service Organizations*. New York: McGraw-Hill, 2016.

Linley. PA and S Joseph. "Positive Change Following Trauma and Adversity: A Review." *Journal of Traumatic Stress*, 17 (2004), 11–21.

Luthans, F, CM Youssef-Morgan, and BJ Avolio. *Psychological Capital and Beyond*. New York: OUP, 2015.

Lynn, M and CR Snyder. "Uniqueness seeking." In *Handbook of Positive Psychology* CR Snyder and SJ Lopez, 395–410. Oxford University Press, 2005.

Maier. SF and MEP Seligman. "Learned Helplessness: Theory and Evidence." *Journal of Experimental Psychology: General*. 105 (1976): 3–46.

Manguel, A. *Curiosity*. New Haven: Yale University Press, 2015.

Media, AH. *Carol Dweck's Mindset: The New Psychology of Success Summary*. New York: Create Space, 2016.

Mintzberg, H. *Bedtime Stories for Managers: Farewell to Lofty Leadership*. New York: Berrett-Koehler, 2019.

Murphy, S. *The Optimistic Workplace*, A;ACON, New York, 2016.

Nakamura, J and M Csikszentmihalyi. "The Concept of Flow." In *Handbook of Positive Psychology*, edited by CR Snyder and SJ Lopez, 89–105. Oxford: Oxford University Press, 2005.

Oswald, A and S Wu. "Objective Confirmation of Subjective Measures of Human Well-Being." *Science*, 327 (2010): 576–579.

Peale, NV. *The Positive Principle Today*. New York: Wings Books, 1994.

124   *Da Vinci motivation as enthusiasm*

Peters, RA. "Effects of Anxiety, Curiosity, and Perceived Instructor Threat on Student verbal Behavior in the College Classroom." *Journal of Educational Psychology*, 70 (1978): 388–395.

Peterson, CM and MEP Seligman. "Positive Organizational Studies: Lessons from Positive Psychology." In *Positive Organizational Scholarship*, edited by KS Cameron, JE Dutton & RE Quinn, 14–29. London: Berret Koehler, BK, 2003.

Peterson, CM, N Park and MEP Seligman. "Orientations to Happiness and Life Satisfaction: The Full Life versus the Empty Life." *Journal of Happiness Studies*, 6 (2005):25–41.

Robertson, I and C Cooper. *Well-Being: Productivity and Happiness at Work*. London: Palgrave Macmillan, 2011.

Ryff,CD and CLM Keyes. "The Structure of Psychological Well-Being revisited." *Journal of Personality and Social Psychology*, 69, no. 4 (1995): 719–727.

Sansone, C and JL Smith. "Interest and Self-Regulation: The Relation between Having to and Wanting To." In *Intrinsic and Extrinsic Motivation*, edited by C Sansone & JM Harackiewicz, 341–372. San Diego, CA: Academic Press, 2000.

Scott, G and A Hoffman. *The Comparing Game*. New York: Create Space, 2015.

Seligman, M. *Helplessness*. San Francisco: Freeman, 1975.

Seligman, M. *Authentic Happiness: Using the New Positive Psychology to Realize Your Potential for Lasting Fulfilment*. New York: Free Press, 2002.

Seligman, M. *Learned Optimism*. New York: Vintage Books, 2006.

Seligman, M. *Flourish: A New Understanding of Happiness and Well-Being*. London: Nicolas Brealey, 2011.

Shipler, DK. *The Working Poor*. New York: Vintage Books, 2005.

Snyder, CP and HL Fromkin. *Uniqueness: The Human Pursuit of Difference*. New York: Plenum, 1980.

Snyder, CR and SJ Lopez. *Positive Psychology: The Scientific and Practical Explorations of Human Strengths*. Thousand Oaks, CA, US: Sage Publications, Inc, 2007.

Sora, B, A Caballer and JM Peiro. "Job insecurity Climate's Influence on Employees Job Attitudes." *European Journal of Work and Organizational Psychology*, 18, no. 2 (2009): 125–147.

Standing, G. *The Precariat: The New Dangerous Class*. New York: Bloomsbury, 2014.

Syed, MC. *Black Box Thinking: Marginal Gains and the Secret of High Performance*. New York: John Murray, 2016.

Thacker, K. *The Art of Authenticity: Tools to Become an Authentic Leader and Your Best Self*. New York: John Wiley & Sons, 2016.

Vallerand, RJ. *The Psychology of Passion: A dualistic Model*. New York: OUP, 2015.

Vogelaar, R. *The Super Promotor: The Power of Enthusiasm.* London: Palgrave, 2010.

Vogelaar, R. Flow: Volume 2 (The enthusiasm trilogy), Super promotor Academy, New York, 2016.

Vogelaar, R. Flame: Volume 1 (The enthusiasm trilogy), Superpromotor Academy, New York, 2016a.

Watzlawick, P, JH Weakland and R Fisch. *Change.* New York: W.W. Norton, 2011.

Wegge, J, HJ Jeppesen, GW Weber, CL Pearce, SA Silva, A Pundt, T Jonsson, S Wolf, CL Wassenaar, C Unterrainer and A Piecha. "Promoting Work Motivation in Organizations: Should Employee Involvement in Organizational Leadership Become a New Tool in the Organizational Psychologist's Kit?." *Journal of Personnel Psychology*, 2010, 9, no. 4 (2010): 154–171, Special Issue: Shared Leadership.

Weich, J. *Mastering the Power of GRIT.* New York: The People Books, 2016.

Wells, AC. "Self-Esteem and Optimal Experience." In *Optimal Experience*, M Csikszentmihalyi and N Csikszentmihalyi, 327–341. Cambridge: Cambridge University Press, 1988.

West, D *Employee Engagement and the Failure of Leadership.* New York: Create Space Independent Publishing, 2012.

Wright, TA. "To Be or Not to Be (Happy): The Role of Employee wellbeing." *Academy of Management Perspectives*, 20 (2006): 118–120.

York, P. *Authenticity Is a Con.* New York: Biteback Publishing, 2014.

Index

Printed in the United States
by Baker & Taylor Publisher Services